CAMBRIDGE LIBRARY COLLECTION

Books of enduring scholarly value

Religion

For centuries, scripture and theology were the focus of prodigious amounts of scholarship and publishing, dominated in the English-speaking world by the work of Protestant Christians. Enlightenment philosophy and science, anthropology, ethnology and the colonial experience all brought new perspectives, lively debates and heated controversies to the study of religion and its role in the world, many of which continue to this day. This series explores the editing and interpretation of religious texts, the history of religious ideas and institutions, and not least the encounter between religion and science.

The Religion of the Manichees

First published in 1924, this volume contains the Donnellan lectures given by Francis Crawford Burkitt (1864–1935) at Trinity College Dublin in June 1923. Their subject is Manichaeism, a dualistic form of Christianity that thrived during the fourth and fifth centuries in Central Asia. Burkitt focuses especially on the discovery of fragments of Manichaean literary texts in Chinese Turkestan, near the Siberian border, early in the twentieth century. The first lecture introduces the history of the Manichees and reviews the sources of information available about them. The second discusses the Manichaean view of Jesus, Manichaean church organisation and Manichaean eschatology. The third analyses the influences behind Manichaean thought and teaching, including the important influences of Marcion and Saint Augustine. Burkitt's lectures were influential in publicising the new finds of Manichaean manuscript fragments, and remain an important resource for those studying heterodox movements in early Christianity.

T0371368

Cambridge University Press has long been a pioneer in the reissuing of out-of-print titles from its own backlist, producing digital reprints of books that are still sought after by scholars and students but could not be reprinted economically using traditional technology. The Cambridge Library Collection extends this activity to a wider range of books which are still of importance to researchers and professionals, either for the source material they contain, or as landmarks in the history of their academic discipline.

Drawing from the world-renowned collections in the Cambridge University Library, and guided by the advice of experts in each subject area, Cambridge University Press is using state-of-the-art scanning machines in its own Printing House to capture the content of each book selected for inclusion. The files are processed to give a consistently clear, crisp image, and the books finished to the high quality standard for which the Press is recognised around the world. The latest print-on-demand technology ensures that the books will remain available indefinitely, and that orders for single or multiple copies can quickly be supplied.

The Cambridge Library Collection will bring back to life books of enduring scholarly value (including out-of-copyright works originally issued by other publishers) across a wide range of disciplines in the humanities and social sciences and in science and technology.

The Religion of
the Manichees

Donnellan Lectures for 1924

Francis Crawford Burkitt

CAMBRIDGE UNIVERSITY PRESS

Cambridge, New York, Melbourne, Madrid, Cape Town, Singapore,
São Paolo, Delhi, Dubai, Tokyo

Published in the United States of America by Cambridge University Press, New York

www.cambridge.org
Information on this title: www.cambridge.org/9781108015264

This edition first published 1925
This digitally printed version 2010

ISBN 978-1-108-01526-4 Paperback

THE RELIGION OF THE MANICHEES

CAMBRIDGE
UNIVERSITY PRESS

LONDON: Fetter Lane

NEW YORK
The Macmillan Co.

BOMBAY, CALCUTTA and
MADRAS
Macmillan and Co., Ltd.

TORONTO
The Macmillan Co. of
Canada, Ltd.

TOKYO
Maruzen-Kabushiki-Kaisha

THE
RELIGION
OF THE
MANICHEES

DONNELLAN
LECTURES FOR
1924

BY

F. C. BURKITT
HON. D.D. (DUBL.)

CAMBRIDGE
AT THE
UNIVERSITY
PRESS
1925

TO THE MOST REVEREND THE PROVOST
AND THE FELLOWS OF TRINITY COLLEGE
DUBLIN I DEDICATE THESE LECTURES
IN GRATEFUL REMEMBRANCE OF MANY
KINDNESSES RECEIVED BOTH RECENTLY
AND IN A PAST GENERATION

PRINTED IN GREAT BRITAIN

PREFACE

THE three Lectures here printed were delivered last June in Trinity College, Dublin, as the Donnellan Lectures for 1924. Their main object is to bring the wonderful discoveries of original Manichee Literature from Central Asia before a wider public than at present seems to know of them, and at the same time to suggest that the Christian element in the Religion of the Manichees is larger and more fundamental than the scholars of the last generation were inclined to allow.

I have to express my very grateful thanks to Prof. Dr A. von Le Coq, Custodian of the Museum für Völkerkunde, Berlin, for his kind permission to me to reproduce two Illustrations from his book *Die Buddhistiche Spätantike in Mittelasien* (2nd Part, *The Manichaean Miniatures*), Berlin, 1923, and to make an adaptation of another for a Title-Page. The Illustration facing p. 1 shews a Wall-Fresco found at Khotscho near Turfan (Chinese Turkestan): the large figure is understood to represent Mani himself, because of the details of the curious head-dress and the elaborate costume. As parts of this figure are faint and mutilated I have made a line-drawing of it as faith-

PREFACE

fully as I could, which will be found facing p. 69. Facing p. 35 is a fragmentary picture, taken from a brightly-coloured illuminated MS., which is believed to represent the Manichaean Sacred Meal or Eucharist, perhaps at the annual Festival of the Chair (*Bema*) of Mani. My Title-Page was the Title-Page of a Manichee Roll: I have attempted to restore the details where they are now torn away in the original. The Uïgur script of the original was written in vertical columns down the central Banner, not across. It is not known for certain what the two Genii stand for, but it may be conjectured that they represent Land and Sky (see p. 54, note).

It is my hope that these Illustrations may lead others, both students of Religion and of Art, to study the admirable reproductions of Manichaean writings and drawings in the series which Prof. v. Le Coq is editing: I am quite sure they are not so well known in this country as they deserve to be.

F. C. BURKITT

CAMBRIDGE
November 1924

CONTENTS

vii

ILLUSTRATIONS

I regret that two interesting studies of some Iranian
elements in Manichaeism by Prof. A. V. Williams Jackson
reached me too late for more than a passing notice here
(*J. of Amer. Oriental Soc.*, vol. 43, pp. 15–25; vol. 44,
pp. 61–72). In the former Article a fresh parallel to
hamōčāg (see p. 105) is given on p. 18. In the latter two
good emendations in the *Fihrist* are proposed, both about
titles of the 'Mother of the Living,' pp. 65, 67. At the
same time I feel that though single details in Manichaeism
can be illustrated or explained from Zoroastrian sources
the fundamental construction of Mani's Religion remains
(heretical) Christian.

MANI, SURROUNDED BY MANICHEE SAINTS.

From a Wall-Fresco found at Khotscho. *See* p. 7.

THE RELIGION OF
THE MANICHEES

· I ·

Sicut pictura cum colore nigro loco suo posito, ita uniuersitas rerum (si quis possit intueri) etiam cum peccatoribus pulchra est, quamuis per se ipsos consideratos sua deformitas turpet.   *De Ciuitate Dei*, xi 23.

THE RELIGION OF THE MANICHEES

I

SUNDAY the 20th of March, A.D. 242, was a holiday in Seleucia-Ctesiphon, for it was the coronation festival of the new King of Kings, Shāpūr I, whose father Ardashir, sixteen years before, had overthrown the Parthians and founded the Sasanian Empire. Shapur himself was destined to reign for over thirty years, to take prisoner in battle a Roman Emperor, to sack the great city of Antioch and look upon the Mediterranean as a conqueror. But the official date of the beginning of his reign is even more memorable as the Pentecost of the Manichaean Religion. It was on the 20th of March, 242, that a young man called Mānī began to announce to the crowds assembled in the streets and bazars of Ctesiphon the new Religion of which he was the Prophet. Such was his success that within a century, in the midst of the decay of Graeco-Roman paganism and the public triumph of Christianity, it seemed to many observers doubtful whether Manichaeism would not overwhelm them both.

Now there are no Manichees left. The new Religion failed to keep a footing in the West, and it has perished in the land of its birth. But it survived for more than a thousand years and only disappeared, like so much that was ancient and interesting, in the age when nearly all Asia and much of Europe was devastated by the Tatar hordes under Zenghis Khan and Tamerlane.

3

I-2

During nearly all that millennium the Manichees were a proscribed and persecuted society, or found a refuge only in outlying regions at the edge of the civilized world. A faith that can command such loyalty must have in it something that corresponds to the needs and aspirations of men and women, something therefore that may be interesting to us. It is from this point of view that I have chosen it as a subject for these Lectures. It is the strange tale of a tragedy of long ago and far away, but I hope it may awake in the end some sympathetic echoes in our thoughts.

I propose to begin by sketching the general outline of the history of the Manichees. This will lead up to a consideration of the literary sources upon which our knowledge of them is based, including the wonderful discoveries of recent years in Central Asia. Finally we shall consider the Manichaean Religion itself, and the philosophy which underlies it.

The message that Mani announced was, in brief, that there are two eternal sources or principles, Light and Dark; that by the regrettable mixture of Dark with Light this visible and tangible Universe has come into being; and that the aim and object of those who are children of Light is not the improvement of this world, for that is impossible, but its gradual extinction, by the separation of the Light particles from the Dark substance with which they have been mixed. To our Western ears this is a melancholy and desperate creed, but it is certain that it possessed a wonderful attraction to the age in which it was first proclaimed.

In 242 Mani was a young man of twenty-six: he was about sixty when Bahrām I, Shapur's grandson, had him executed. Mani's corpse, or his flayed skin stuffed with hay, was set up over one of the gates of the royal city of Gundē-Shapur, east of Susa, which in consequence was known for centuries as the Mānī-gate. Bahram also proscribed Mani's religion and attempted to root it out altogether, but after a whole generation of missionary effort it had become well established all through the East, and persecution only drove it below the surface. Four hundred years later, when the Sasanian Empire, exhausted by long wars with Constantinople, fell before the vigour of the Arab conquerors, the Persian dominions were honeycombed with Manichees. No doubt at first the change must have been to them a great relief. The first generation of Arabs were probably unaware of their existence. Persecution directed against Unbelievers concerned in the first instance the Zoroastrian Fire-worshippers, under which the old national Religion of the Persians, now disestablished and harassed with vexatious regulations, sank into obscurity. But as soon as the existence of Manichees became known to Moslem rulers of every sort they were ruthlessly suppressed wherever they were discovered.

No continuous history of the Manichees can be written. All we know from Mohammedan sources is that from time to time Manichees—Arabic writers call them *Zindīḳs*—were detected, ruined, killed, and held up to execration. They were considered by Moslems not merely Unbelievers, the followers of a False Prophet, but unnatural and unsocial, a danger to the State. Yet the author of the *Fihrist*, who lived at the end of the 10th century, tells us that he had been acquainted with about 300 Manichees in Baghdad alone. All these, of course, were Manichees in secret: neither in Christian nor in Mohammedan lands was Manichaeism a *religio licita*. But Al-Bīrūnī, writing about the year 1000 A.D., says that "most of the eastern Turks, of the people of China and Thibet, and some of the Hindus, adhere to Mani's law and doctrine[1]." In the *Fihrist* we read that the Manichees were tolerated about the same period in Samarkand, because the "King of China"—probably, says our author, it was the Chief of the Taghazghaz[2] Turks—had threatened reprisals if they were killed. The Taghazghaz lived in Chinese Turkestan, east of Kashgar, round about the lake or inland sea called on our maps Lop Nor.

These statements of ancient writers were verified

[1] Sachau, p. 191.
[2] This is the name given in Arabic sources, such as the *Fihrist*. It is a corruption of *Toquz Oghuz*, *i.e.* 'The Nine Clans.' See A. von Le Coq, *Manichaica* III (1922), p. 40.

in the early years of this century in a surprising and most satisfactory fashion. Three or four scientific expeditions were made to Chinese Turkestan, and some thousands of fragments of MSS. were discovered and brought back to Europe, especially from the neighbourhood of a town called Turfan. Some hundreds of these fragments are from Manichaean MSS., written in the peculiar script used by the Manichees, so that we now know something about them from their own writings, and not only from the refutations of their adversaries. Unfortunately these newly-found documents are all scraps, bits of torn books and rolls, and written in languages as yet imperfectly known. Were it not for our other sources of information, from Mohammedan and Christian opponents, we should be unable to understand the allusions in the Turfan documents.

Let us now glance at the history of Manichaeism in the Roman Empire. Here again no continuous account can be given, and some of the chief sources of information most used by Christians about the Manichees seem to have been semi-fabulous. But certain incidents stand out with startling vividness. One episode in particular may be told in full in the words of an eye-witness. Mark, deacon to S. Porphyry of Gaza, is prejudiced and superstitious and no doubt he writes some years after the events he describes, but his account of the Manichee missionary who came to Gaza about the year 400 shews us the movement as a living and active religion.

About that time (says Mark[1]) there came to sojourn in the city [of Gaza] a certain woman of Antioch called Julia, who was of the abominable heresy of them which are called Manichaeans; and knowing that certain persons were but lately enlightened and not yet stablished in the holy faith she wrought secretly and corrupted them, bewitching them by her doctrine, and much more by gifts of money. For he that invented the said godless heresy was not able to catch any otherwise than by the bestowing of money. For unto those who have understanding their doctrine is filled full of all blasphemy and condemnation and old wives' fables that entice foolish womenfolk and childish men of vain mind and wit. For out of divers heresies and opinions of the Greeks did they build up this their evil belief, desiring by wickedness and craft to take hold on all men. For they say that there be many gods, that they may be acceptable unto the Greeks; and moreover they acknowledge nativities and fate and the science of the stars, in order that they may sin without fear, holding that the commission of sins is not in us, but cometh from the necessity of fate. (86) But they confess Christ also, for they say that he was made man in appearance; for they themselves in appearance are called Christians.... For even as a painter making a mixture of divers colours perfecteth the appearance of a man or a beast or some other thing for the deceit of them that behold it, that it may seem to them that are foolish and without understanding to be true, but to them that have understanding it is a shadow and a deceit and an invention of man; so also the Manichaeans having drawn out of divers opinions did perfect their own evil belief, nay rather, having gathered together and mingled the venom of divers serpents, did prepare a deadly poison for the destruction of the souls of men. But, as aforesaid, that pestilent woman having come to the city, certain persons

---

[1] Mark the Deacon, 85–91: I quote from the admirable translation of G. F. Hill.

were led away by her deceitful teaching. (87) But after some days Saint Porphyry, having been informed by certain of the believers, sent for her and questioned her, who she was and whence and what manner of belief she held. And she confessed both her country and that she was a Manichaean. And when they that stood around him were moved with wrath (for there were certain devout men with him), the blessed man besought them not to be angered, but with patience to exhort her a first and a second time, observing the saying of the holy Apostle (Tit. iii 10). Then saith he to the woman: "Abstain, Sister, from this evil belief, for it is of Satan." But she answered: "Speak and hear, and either persuade or be persuaded." And the blessed man said: "Prepare thyself against the morrow and present thyself here." So she took her leave and departed. But the blessed man, having fasted and prayed much unto Christ that he would shame the devil, prepared himself against the next day and called certain of the devout, both clergy and laymen, to hear the dispute between himself and the woman. (88) And on the morrow the woman presenteth herself, having with her two men and as many women; they were young and fair to look upon, and the faces of them all were pale; but Julia was old in years. And they all did build their reasoning upon the teaching of this world, and much more Julia than the others. And their guise was lowly and their manner gentle, but, as it is said, they were outwardly sheep and inwardly ravening wolves and venomous beasts; for hypocrisy is in all their words and deeds. Then being bidden to sit down they inquired into the matter. And the saint, holding the holy gospels and having made the sign of the Cross on his mouth, began to ask her to declare her belief and she began to speak. And brother Cornelius the deacon, being skilled in the short-hand of Ennomus, did at the bidding of the most blessed bishop note all that was said and disputed, I and brother Barochas reminding him.

I am sorry to say that Mark now explains that he did not write the dispute in this book, "seeing that it was long," so that we have no report of "the old wives' fables which the marvel-monger and magician Julia spake in her foolishness." The end was dramatic. Mark goes on to say (89):

After she had said many vain things for many hours and spoken the customary blasphemies against the Lord and God of all, Saint Porphyry, being moved by divine zeal, when he saw Him that comprehendeth all things both seen and unseen blasphemed by a woman possessed of the devil and submitting herself to his will, gave forth his sentence against her, saying: "God, who made all things, who alone is eternal, having neither beginning nor ending, who is glorified in trinity, shall smite thy tongue and muzzle thy mouth, that thou mayest not speak evil things." (90) And straightway with the sentence followed also the punishment; for Julia began to tremble and her countenance to be changed, and continuing as in a trance for a certain time she spake not, but was without voice or motion, having her eyes open and fastened upon the most holy bishop. But they that were with her, beholding that which she suffered, were sore afraid, and sought to awake her spirit and sang charms into her ear; and there was no speech and there was no hearing. And after she had been for a certain time without speech, she gave up the ghost, departing unto the darkness which she honoured, holding it to be light.

Bishop Porphyry had the old lady properly buried: "he was exceeding compassionate," says Mark, who adds that the men and women who had appeared with Julia confessed their error. "(91) But the blessed man caused them all to curse Manes, the author of their heresy, after whom also they were called Manichaeans, and having instructed them for many days he brought them into the holy Catholic Church."

Poor Julia! I have quoted this story almost in

full, because it gives us so much of the fear and animosity with which the Manichaean Religion was regarded during the centuries when it was a crusading, missionary Faith.

The Manichaean propaganda when at its height was not stopped by barriers of language or culture. It had spread by the middle of the 4th century into the Latin-speaking West, and in Carthage it secured its most famous convert. For nine years, from 373 onwards, Augustine was a Manichee and in various ways the Manichaean Religion left an enduring impress on his mind, relics of which can still be traced in actually current notions. Certainly in the contrasted conceptions of the *Ciuitas Dei* and the *Ciuitas Mundi* there is a perceptible reflexion of the Manichee notion of the eternal realms of Light and Dark.

The experience that S. Augustine had had served him well when as a Bishop in Africa he had to withstand Manichee missionaries such as Fortunatus and Felix, or to confute Manichee books of controversy such as that of Faustus. Several of Augustine's works still remain among our chief authorities for the doctrines of Manichaeism. But after Augustine's day, that is, from the middle of the 5th century onwards, our information is very scanty. It is all the scantier if account be taken of the fact that orthodox Christians often used the word 'Manichaean' to describe heretics whose doctrines were imperfectly understood but seemed to impugn the goodness of God or the salvability of the human body. The Bogomils of Bulgaria, the 'Cathari' and 'Patarenes' of Lombardy, and above all the Albigensians, have often been called Manichees in ancient and modern times. It is likely that fragments of their teaching were really derived from Manichaean sources. But now that we have so much more exact knowledge of what the Religion of the Manichees really was I think it misleading to call these sects, even the Albigensians, by the name of Manichees. In any case it is hazardous to use Albigensian material to illustrate the Religion we are studying.

The chief authorities on which our knowledge of Manichaeism is based may be grouped in a geographical order. Beginning with the West, we have in Latin the writings of S. Augustine, with which must be associated the *De Fide* ascribed to Augustine's friend Evodius.

In Greek there are many polemics against the Manichees, but when looked at carefully it is clear that the writers are all dependent on a very few original authorities. These are (in addition to Mark the Deacon, quoted above): (1) Alexander of Lycopolis; (2) the Acts of Archelaus, by 'Hegemonius' (see below); (3) Titus of Bostra; (4) Severus of Antioch, Homily cxxiii, extant only in Syriac translations; (5) the Formula of Abjuration, which converted Manichees had to pronounce before reception into the Church (Migne, *P.G.* 1, 1461–9):

this document in its present form dates only from the 9th century, but it preserves with a good deal of fidelity certain names and religious expressions.

Epiphanius writes copiously against the Manichees in his *Panarion*, Heresy 66 (or 46), but he is dependent on the Acts of Archelaus and on Titus of Bostra. The great service he has rendered is to quote in full the general account of the Manichaean Religion given in the Acts of Archelaus, a work otherwise extant only in a Latin translation. This general account is the kernel of the whole work, the only part of it which has any scientific value.

In Syriac we have the anti-Manichaean writings of S. Ephraim who died in 373, only a century after Mani himself. Certain polemical discourses in verse by this Church Father have long been known, but the numerous bitter words contained in them against Mani were too vague and allusive to be of much value to the modern investigator. Since 1921 we have the two volumes of the late C. W. Mitchell's decipherment of Ephraim's prose *Refutations of Mani, Marcion and Bardaisan*, taken from a 6th century MS. in the British Museum which is mostly palimpsest and very difficult to read[1]. S. Ephraim, for our purposes, is a very tiresome writer; he is exceedingly prolix, while

[1] *S. Ephraim's Prose Refutations of Mani, Marcion and Bardaisan....* by C. W. Mitchell, vol. I, 1912; vol. II, 1921 (quoted as Mitchell, I and II). Mr Mitchell was a young Canadian scholar, trained at Cambridge, who was killed in France in 1917 when on active service as a Chaplain.

only making the smallest possible direct quotations from his heretical adversaries. But with all drawbacks his work appears to me to be of very great importance. He writes in Syriac, in the language in which most of Mani's own writings were composed, so that the terms and titles by which he names the technicalities of Manichee Religion are likely to be Mani's own names for them. But further, I venture to think that Ephraim's diagnosis of Manichaeism is in essence more correct than a great deal that has been written on it by modern scholars, for he regards it as mainly a mixture of the heretical systems of Marcion and of Bardaisan. No doubt this is not all the truth: there is doubtless a large non-Christian element in the Manichee Religion, but its Christian parts do seem to me to have greater affinity with the Christianity of Marcion and of Bardaisan than with that of the Catholic Church, and these parts seem to me to be the living kernel of the Manichaean system.

Besides Ephraim we have in Syriac the *Book of Scholia* by Theodore bar Khoni (or rather, Konai[1]), Nestorian Bishop of Kashkar[2], who seems to have lived at the beginning of the 7th century. Theodore, fortunately for us, quotes directly from a Manichaean writing, so that his witness, though com-

---

[1] The name (ܟܘܢܝ) is vocalized *Konai* in *C.U.L.* Add. 1998 (*Cat. of Camb. U. Libr.*, p. 444).

[2] Kashkar, not to be confounded with Kashgar in Turkestan (see p. 6), was a town or district in Lower Babylonia, now called Wāsit.

paratively late, is of special value. The *Scholia* are given with a full and illuminating commentary in Franz Cumont's *Cosmogonie Manichéenne*, which is vol. I of his *Recherches sur le Manichéisme*[1].

In Arabic the most important accounts of Mani and the Manichaean literature are that by Al-Bīrūnī, and the work called the *Fihrist* (or Catalogue) by Mohammed ibn Ishāk al-Warrāk, known as An-Nadīm. This latter work, the *Fihrist al-'ulūm*, a sort of History of Literature, contains a long chapter on Mani and his writings, which is one of the most detailed and most accurate sources we possess on the subject: it was admirably edited and translated with copious explanatory notes by Gustav Flügel in 1862[2]. The *Fihrist* was written in 988 A.D., and Al-Bīrūnī's work about 1000 A.D.

Finally we have the Manichaean fragments discovered early in this century in Chinese Turkestan. In these, and these only, we hear Manichees speaking for themselves and not through the reports of adversaries. Unfortunately the fragments consist almost entirely of small and often unintelligible scraps, and they are written either in the Soghdian language, *i.e.* a sort of Middle-Persian intermediate between the Old-Persian of the inscriptions and the language used to-day, or

---

[1] Published in 1908. Here quoted as Cumont, I. The Severus Homily is quoted as Cumont, II.

[2] *Mani, seine Lehre und seine Schriften*, von G. Flügel (quoted as Flügel by its pages).

else in a Proto-Turkish which bears a somewhat similar relation to the speech of Constantinople and Angora. Other documents bearing on the Manichees and coming from the same region are in Chinese.

Further, the texts and translations of the fragments have to be sought for in many different publications. Prof. F. W. K. Müller and Prof. A. von Le Coq write in the *Sitzungsberichte* and *Abhandlungen* of the Berlin Academy, MM. Chavannes and Pelliot in the *Journal Asiatique* of Paris. Some other documents were published by Prof. Salemann in the *Proceedings* of the (then) Imperial Academy of Petersburg, and one very important text, the Khuastuanift, has been most fully published by v. Le Coq in the *Journal of the Royal Asiatic Society* for 1911 from a roll discovered by Sir Aurel Stein. It is fortunate that for everything published before 1918 we have an admirable guide to these newly-found texts in M. Prosper Alfaric's *Écritures Manichéennes*, a work to which I am much indebted[1].

Before attempting to criticise the Religion of the Manichees, to estimate its influence, its merits and defects, it is necessary to describe it. In what follows I have been somewhat eclectic, but I give references to the authorities wherever it seems necessary.

From all our sources, from Augustine in the

[1] See especially I, pp. 129–138; II, pp. 126–136.

West to the Manichaean penitential Litany in the far North-East, we learn that the Manichees began with the Two Roots, and to this was added the Three Moments. The Two Roots, or Principles, are those of the Light and the Dark; by the Three Moments they mean the Past, the Present and the Future[1]. Light and Dark are two absolutely different eternal Existences. In the beginning they were separate, as they should be. But in the *Past* the Dark made an incursion on the Light and some of the Light became mingled with the Dark, as it still is in the *Present*; nevertheless a means of refining this Light from the Dark was called into being and of protecting the whole realm of Light from any further invasion, so that in the *Future* the Light and the Dark will be happily separated.

Light and Dark are the proper designations of the two Principles, but conjoined with the idea of the Light was everything that was Good, orderly, peaceful, intelligent; with that of the Dark everything that was Bad, anarchic, turbulent, material. "The difference between these two Principles is like that between a King and a Pig: Light dwells in a royal abode in places suitable to its nature, while the Dark like a pig wallows in mud and is nourished by filth and delights in it[2]." Another expression of this fundamental

---

[1] See Alfaric, II 66, and the *Khuastuanift* (quoted below).

[2] Cumont, II 97, a quotation from Severus, who is quoting a work of Mani, very probably that called *Kephalaia* in Greek and *Do Bun* (*i.e.* 'Two Roots') in Persian.

dualism is that of the Two Trees, the Tree of Life or Good Tree, and the Tree of Death[1]. These are regarded as filling all Space, and the way this is described lets us see Mani's view of the relative amounts of Light and Dark that he conceived to exist. In effect three-quarters of Space, all that extends to East and West and North, is the undisputed realm of the Tree of Life. The Tree of Death is only in the Southern quarter. There the Tree of Life also exists, but it is invisible, shrouded from alien gaze by what is variously called its own 'glory' and a 'wall' raised by 'God' for its protection[2]. We may fairly infer from this curious passage that Mani thought of the Light as at least more than three times as great and powerful as the Dark nature[3]. Also we may believe that this placing of the evil burning black Nature in the South is a thought that had its origin in the hot plains of Babylonia.

The most usual Manichaean presentation of the primordial condition of the Light and the Dark is that of two contiguous Realms or States, existing side by side from all eternity without any commixture. Each Realm was self-contained and appropriately organized. In the Realm of Light dwelt the Father of Greatness with his Light, his Power, and his Wisdom, forming a sort of

---

[1] Cumont, II 96, 100 f. [2] *Ibid.* II 100–105.

[3] If in the comparatively 'dark' realm of the South the 'dark' be thought of as twice as great as the 'light,' then on the whole the 'light' will be five times as great as the 'dark.'

Quaternity which the Greek Manichees called 'Four-Faced[1].' This Supreme Ruler of Light was rendered *Zrvān* by the Persian-speaking Manichees, just as we sometimes speak of God as 'The Eternal.' Mani represents the Father of Greatness as occupying five Dwellings: we should say five Attributes, for the word is the Syriac form of the Hebrew *Shekinah*. These five are Sense, Reason, Thought, Imagination, Intention[2]—the qualities of a sane and intelligent mind.

Opposite this blissful Realm or *terra lucida*, as S. Augustine calls it, is the Realm of the Dark, inhabited by the King of the Dark with his restless and infernal brood, a region of suffocating smoke, of destructive fire, of scorching wind, of poisonous water, of "darkness which may be felt[3]." I use the familiar phrase from Exodus, though not expressly quoted in our documents, because it brings out the substantial character of the 'Dark' as imagined by the Manichees. We, following Aristotle and Milton, know that darkness is

Privation mere of light and absent day[4],

[1] Manichee converts to Catholicism had to abjure τὸν τετραπρόσωπον Πατέρα τοῦ Μεγέθουσ (*Abjuration*, 1461): see Cumont, I 8.

[2] The five Syriac words are ܗܘܢܐ, ܡܕܥܐ, ܪܢܝܐ, ܡܚܫܒܬܐ, ܬܪܥܝܬܐ. There is a good Note on them by Kugener in Cumont, I 10. For the renderings here adopted see the separate Note at the end of this chapter (p. 33).

[3] Theodore b. Konai in Cumont, I 11, note.

[4] *Paradise Regained*, IV 400: see J. E. B. Mayor's Catena of passages from Augustine and others in illustration of this phrase (*Journal of Philology*, 1903, No. 56, pp. 289–292).

but to the Manichees it was something positive. The Syriac word for 'darkness' (*ḥeššōχā*) is not an abstract, but rather the Dark substance or place[1], as indeed it seems to be in Hebrew, for to the Psalmist darkness could be 'sent[2].' We shall see later on that Mani did not invent this substantial quality of his 'darkness,' but took it over from a previous philosophy.

The denizens of this pestiferous Realm suited its character. Mani represents them as groping about in aimless anarchy, at enmity with each other, so far as they were aware of each other's existence. He was evidently at pains to represent the Realm of Darkness as being in every way odious. But we have not yet come to anything that can properly be described as Evil. The horrible Dark is peopled with a horrible race appropriate in character and habits to the place they live in. Evil began when the Dark invaded the Light.

Mani naturally could not explain how this first disturbance of the eternal order took place, but he seems somewhere to have expressed it, that it was as if the Dark from a far distance smelt and perceived that there was "something pleasant" beyond his region[3]. Here, as elsewhere in many ancient religions, a conception which has its true

[1] As we say 'in *the* dark' in English.
[2] Psalm cv 28. It seems something of a marvel to the Fourth Evangelist that 'darkness' cannot 'take hold of' light (John i 5).
[3] Mitchell, I, p. lx.

root in human nature is expressed and believed in as a cosmological happening, for I cannot doubt that Mani's point is, that the beginning of Evil is unregulated desire.

But we must not philosophize at this early stage, still less regard Mani's cosmological revelations as allegories. Fantastic as Mani's Gods or Angels may be, it is clear that he and his disciples believed in them as real. The modern investigator has to be careful on both sides: to be fair to the Religion of the Manichees we need to remember that the fantastic myths which Mani taught correspond to a serious view of the strange mixture of good and bad, which we feel within ourselves and see in other human beings; and on the other hand as historians we must not treat as allegories the tales of the Primal Man and the rest of the Manichaean mythology because to us with our modern scientific conceptions of the material universe they sound silly and bizarre.

To this tale of the Primal Man we must now come. The tale is indeed fundamental to Manichaeism. According to Mani, writing to one Patticius[1], it is useless to consider the origin of Adam and Eve till one has understanding of "what happened before the constitution of the world, and how the War broke out, so as to be

---

[1] *Patticius* in Latin, Πατέκιοσ in Greek. Flügel, and others following him, spell this name *Futtak*, but the 'u' only rests on the vocalization of one of Flügel's MSS. of the *Fihrist*. Shahrastānī has *Fātik*.

able to separate the nature of Light from the Dark[1]." The story is told in the fullest detail by Theodore bar Konai, in whose account, as it is written in Syriac, the various personages are spoken of by their original Manichaean names[2].

The trouble began by the Ruler of the Dark coming up out of his domain to invade the realms of Light. Thus the great event, to the issue of which is due the existence of this world we live in, came to pass through the unlicensed initiative of the Powers of Darkness. The invasion caused consternation in all the Five Realms of Light, for they were unprovided with defences. "In the world of Light there is no burning Fire such as could be hurled against the Evil One, no cutting Iron or suffocating Water, nor any other evil thing of the sort; everything there is Light and a free region[3]." The Father of Greatness, who saw that His existing Manifestations (or *Shekinahs*) were unable to resist the Enemy, "for they had been created for tranquillity and peace," decided to oppose the Powers of Darkness by a new kind of Being. So "the Father of Greatness evoked the Mother of Life, and the Mother of Life evoked the Primal Man[4]."

Two points call for notice in passing. It must not be supposed that the Primal Man is Adam:

[1] Ap. Aug. *c. Ep. Fundamenti*, 12.
[2] For what follows, see Cumont, I 13 ff.
[3] Severus, ap. Cumont, II 127.
[4] Cumont, I 14: the Syriac is ܟܝ݂ܢܐ ܟܐܝܟ.

he is more like the πρῶτοσ ἄνθρωποσ which appears in some Gnostic speculations[1] in that he is wholly Divine, consubstantial with the Father of Greatness, and so is consistently invoked as God in prayer and praise in Manichee Hymns. He is 'consubstantial,' but not 'begotten.' As we shall see, Manichaeism was always ascetic, even to the terms in which Mani expressed his cosmology. All generation was to Mani hateful, for it was a fresh mixture. To take life was to cut the Parts of the Light imprisoned in a living body; to produce fresh life was to perpetuate a state of things that ought never to have been. It was equally wrong to sow and to reap, and the Elect Manichees—the Righteous (zaddīkē), as they called themselves— were not willing even to break bread lest they should pain the Light which is mixed with it (Mitchell, I, p. xxx), their food, as we learn from other sources, being wholly prepared for them by mere disciples[2]. In accordance with this the Manichaeans appear to have avoided all words like 'beget,' or even 'create,' in describing the production of the Hierarchy of Light. We hear of the Father of Greatness and the Mother of Life (or, of the Living), but the Primal Man is not styled their Son: Mani seems to have carried through the idea of the Logos, or mere Word, as the producing organ. The Father of Greatness neither espouses the Mother of Life nor begets the Primal

[1] See Iren. *Haer.* i 30, 1.
[2] *Acta Archelai*, ix ad fin.

Man, but calls (ܪܚ̈ܡܐ)—and they exist[1]. The word is not a dialectical peculiarity, but a theological idiom. There is no syzygy of the Aeons in Manichaeism, as in the system of Valentinus. Moreover there is this fundamental difference between Manichaean and Christian Theology, whether Catholic or Gnostic, that the Trinity or the Ogdoad are set forth as primordial, if not eternal: the resulting Hierarchy or Divine Society is the natural outcome of the ultimate Divine Being, and therefore terms of generation were used, in order to avoid the impression that the 'Son' of God was in any way made out of something else. But in Manichaean Theology the Divine Hierarchy was not eternal; it was, like everything else we know of, the result of the initiative of Evil, a by-product of unregulated Desire.

The Primal Man having been called into being, he was clothed or armed for the fight with the Five Bright Elements, called in Syriac the *Zīwānē*. That these were five in number is constantly asserted; in fact, the Turkish-speaking Manichees seem to have invoked these Elements by the curious name of 'Five-God.' But though four of the five were certainly Light, Wind, Fire and Water, there is some uncertainty as to what was the fifth. Augustine (*c. Faust.* II 3) seems to give *aer*, the *Acta Archelai* (ap. Epiph. 659) have ὕλη, the *Fihrist* gives 'the gentle breeze' (النسيم). I may

---

[1] Similarly Cumont, I 14.

add that the Soghdian word seems to be *pravaḥr* and the Uïgur Turkish *tïntura*, conventionally rendered 'aether[1].'

However this may be, the Primal Man, armed or clothed with his Five Bright Elements and preceded by an angel called Naḥashbaṭ, bearing a crown of victory, went forth to repel the King of the Dark. But the result was disaster. The Primal Man was left lying unconscious on the field of battle, and the Five Bright Elements were swallowed up by the Dark, which itself is sometimes regarded as a single King of Darkness, sometimes as a plurality, the Sons of the Dark, also called by Manichees the Archons[2]. This all-important combat was sometimes represented in Manichaean documents as not altogether a victory for the Dark. The Primal Man, it is true, was left lying unconscious and his *Zīwānē* were swallowed up, but both Ephraim (Mitchell, I, p. lxxix) and Titus of Bostra (A 17) tell us that the *Zīwānē* were used by the Primal Man as a bait (δέλεαρ) to catch the Sons of the Dark. The idea was, they tell us, that the infernal Powers were weakened by having some sweetness and light mingled with their substance.

When the Primal Man recovered from his swoon, he entreated the Father of Greatness to come to his support. So a second creation, or

[1] See Appendix II.
[2] In Syriac ܐܪܟܘܢ (pl. ܐܪܟܘܢܐ). The word, derived from the Greek ἄρχων, possibly occurs even in the Turkish *Khuastuanift*, l. 169.

rather evocation, of Light-powers came into being, which were the Friend of the Luminaries, the Great Ban and the Living Spirit[1]. What the Friend of the Luminaries did is not quite certain: possibly he was responsible for making the Sun and Moon. We learn from Ephraim that Ban was the Architect who planned the Walls that were ultimately to confine the Powers of Darkness in their infernal region, while Theodore b. Konai tells us that the Living Spirit produced the five heavenly Powers that hold our mixed world together.

But our world was not yet formed, according to the Manichaean cosmogony. We have not yet come to the mastering of the Dark Power by the Light. And indeed how exactly this came about our accounts do not make clear, except that the power of the Living Spirit (so Theodore) or of the Friend of the Luminaries (so the *Fihrist*, p. 88) restored to the Primal Man his divine energy. He had lost his panoply, and was swallowed up in the region of the Dark, but he himself was unharmed and unpolluted. And so he descended to the lowest deep of the Abyss and cut the roots of the Five dark Elements, so that they could never increase[2]. Then he returned to the field

[1] Cumont, I 21.
[2] This detail, so far as I know, is only preserved in the *Fihrist* (Flügel, p. 89). I accept it here for three reasons: (1) the Roots correspond to the Myth of the Two Trees, mentioned above; (2) the tale recurs, with characteristic differences, in the *Book of Hierotheos*; and (3) it appears to be a mythical expansion of Eph. iv 9, 10.

of battle and took the Powers of Darkness prisoner.

Thus the primordial invasion of the Light by the Dark anarchic Powers was definitely arrested. But as we now all know, Victory is one thing and Reparations another. The dark Archons were defeated and captured, but they had absorbed—in point of fact, digested—the Five bright Elements, and the Realm of Light would be for ever poorer if these were not recovered. The problem now was not only how to turn the proper region of Darkness into a prison by encircling it with an impenetrable Wall, but also how to extract the absorbed Light from the Archons. According to Mani our world is the result of this process.

First of all, a great deal of the Light-substance was immediately disgorged, and of this the two pure Luminaries, Sun and Moon, were made, together with all they required in their course through the heavens[1]. But a great deal remained in the very frames of the Archons, so the Primal Man (as Ephraim tells us)[2] "flayed them, and made this Sky from their skins, and out of their excrement he compacted the Earth, and out of their bones he moulded and raised and piled up the Mountains," so that "in rain and dew the pure Elements yet remaining in them might be squeezed out." Thus to Mani our earth with the visible heavens

---

[1] See Müller, II (1904), p. 38 f.
[2] Mitchell, I, p. xxxiii f.

above us is formed of the dismembered parts of the evil demons of Darkness. And how, we ask, is it held together and kept in its place? That, we are told, is the task of the Five Beings evoked by the Living Spirit. There is the *Splenditenens*, as Augustine calls him (*c. Faust.* xx 10), who holds the world suspended like a chandelier[1]; the 'King of Honour,' whose rays collect the fragments of the light-particles; the 'Adamant,' with his shield and spear driving off any rescue-party of the demons of the Dark; the 'King of Glory,' who rotates the heavenly spheres that surround the world; and finally the gigantic 'Atlas,' on whose shoulders the whole mass is supported.

The damage done by the invasion of the Realms of Light was thus localized. The Archons, within whose bodies some particles of Light had been absorbed, are held in their place, and now the Heavenly Powers supplicate the Eternal, the 'Father of Greatness,' to evoke some means of extracting these remaining particles. First He had evoked the Primal Man, then the Living Spirit, and now He sends a Third Creation, the *Legatus*

[1] The names are given by Theodore (Cumont, I 22, note) in the original Syriac. Of these the ‫ܩܠܡܘ‬, or 'Supporter,' is mentioned by Ephraim (Mitchell, II 208₃₉ = p. xcviii), and the *Splenditenens* in the preceding line. Unfortunately the first part of this latter name is illegible in the MS. Theodore gives ‫ܨܡܚ ܐܘܢ‬: I have conjectured that this is to be connected with Assyr. *ṣabit*, Ar. *ḍābiṭ*, and Jewish Aramaic צביתא, so that the meaning will be 'Tongs of Brilliance.'

Tertius, the native name for whom was *Īzgaddā*, the Messenger.

There was an old myth, used by some of the Christian Gnostics, which told how Barbelo, the great Goddess of Gnostic lore, shewed her beauty to the 'Archons,' who became enamoured of her and thereby emitted their 'power[1].' This notion appears in various forms and may very likely be the survival of some antique nature-myth. The myth was borrowed by Mani, and applied to the Messenger and his attendants, for he appeared to the captive Archons as a beautiful person of the opposite sex to each of them, and they in a passion of desire began to give out the Light which they had absorbed from the *Zīwānē*, or Light-elements. But with the Light came out also the 'sin' which was engrained in their substance, whereupon the Messenger hid himself from them and separated the Light that had emanated from the Archons from the 'sinful' part. The Light was rescued and taken up into the Sun and Moon, while the 'sin' fell on the earth, partly on the sea, partly on the dry land. That which fell on the sea turned into a horrible monster, the image of the King of the Dark, but Adamas was ready and transfixed his heart with his great lance[2]. That which fell on the dry land turned into Trees, and so living plants

[1] Epiphanius, *Haer.* xxv 2 (on the 'Nicolaitans'): see Cumont, I 67.

[2] In other words, exactly like S. George and the Dragon. Only the Horse is absent.

came into being. The 'sin' of which they are made is, in fact, according to Manichaean notions, the sinful substance which ought never to have come into being, *viz.* a mixture of the Dark substance with the Elements of Light. The strange tale which Mani gave of the origin of plants lent itself to obscene deductions, which Christian controversialists were not slow to make, but I think that M. Cumont has sufficiently demonstrated that the myth, as used by Mani, was consciously 'volatilisé' (p. 67). The reason why the 'Messenger' must be introduced in any account of the Manichaean cosmogony is that he is the heavenly prototype of the later, human Messengers of the Powers of Light, the *Prēstags* and *Burkbāns*, such finally as was Mani himself. These Messengers of the Light, accompanied by their virtues, come to men and are the main agents whereby the remaining Light in this dark world is to become separated and rescued from its surroundings.

The creation of animals followed in a somewhat similar manner, and the Archons began to fear that all the Light that they had absorbed would be conjured out of them. So, by a strange process of generation and cannibalism, the King of the Dark caused his infernal spouse to give birth to a fresh being in which was hidden most of the absorbed Light. This was Adam. He was made 'in the image of God,' that is to say in the image of the Divine Messenger who had appeared to the Archons. The same parents afterwards produced

Eve, but she had in her frame less of the Light. Adam, on the other hand, was truly a microcosm, the image of the universe, of God and matter, of Light and Dark.

So Jesus, the *Zīwānā*,—I cannot here discuss this epithet[1], but in any case it means a heavenly Being,—was sent down to earth, where Adam was lying inert on the ground. Jesus, called by Manichees the Friend[2], found him plunged in deep sleep, awoke him, made him move, aroused him from his slumber, and drove away the demons that watched over him. Then Adam looked at himself and knew what he was[3]. Jesus shewed Adam some at least of the Heavenly Hierarchy, and made him realize that though he, Jesus, was in essence wholly of the Light, the Light in this world is exposed to all sorts of dangers, to be torn by wild beasts, eaten by dogs, always being mixed and imprisoned in the foul substances that are derived from the Dark[4]. In this way Adam comes to a knowledge of his true nature. "Jesus made him stand upright and taste of the Tree of Life. Then Adam looked and wept, he lifted up his voice like a roaring lion, he tore

[1] See Appendix II.
[2] Cumont, I 46, last line (*cet ami*). The epithet 'Friend' (*'ariyâmân*) for the heavenly Jesus is found in Manichaean texts from Turfan: see Müller, II ('04), p. 28.
[3] Theodore, ap. Cumont, I 46 f.: Cumont points out that what is explained to Adam is the doctrine of the 'suffering Jesus' that we find among the African Manichees.
[4] *Ibid.* 48.

his hair and beat his breast, and said: 'Woe, woe, to the creator of my body! Woe to him who has bound my soul to it, and to the rebels who have brought me to servitude!'"

This is the last of the Manichaean extracts quoted by Theodore bar Konai. M. Cumont adds: "By making Adam taste of the fruit of knowledge Jesus, and not the Tempter, revealed to him the depth of his misery. But man will know henceforth the way of enfranchisement. He must consecrate his life to keeping his soul from all corporal defilement by practising continence and renunciation, so as to set free little by little from the bonds of matter the Divine Substance within him and disseminated throughout nature, and thereby join in the great work of distillation which God is occupied with in the Universe[1]."

M. Cumont points out that the passage about Adam quoted above was probably part of the peroration of the *Epistula Fundamenti*, against which S. Augustine polemizes, the Letter of Mani known as 'the Great Epistle to Patticius,' also called, as M. Alfaric has made probable, by the Greek name πραγματεία[2].

We have been dealing all this time with what the Manichees thought of the *Past*: in the next Lecture we shall consider their ideas on the *Present* and the *Future*. Of the Past there is little more to be said. According to Mani, Adam,

[1] Cumont, I 49.   [2] Alfaric, II 58–68.

warned in time, kept away from Eve for a long period, for neither Cain nor Abel was his son; they were both sons of the Archon-brood. At last, however, Adam forgot his duty and so Seth (or, as the Manichees called him, *Shēthil*[1]) was born, and in him and his descendants the particles of the Light are still imprisoned.

[1] شاثل: see Flügel, p. 269. The name is also found among the Mandaeans.

NOTE ON THE FIVE ATTRIBUTES (p. 19)

The five Syriac words quoted on p. 19, note 2, are often rendered 'mind' or 'thought' somewhat indiscriminately: their more exact meaning may be inferred from the following examples:

Haunā (ܗܘܢܐ) is *Sense* or Sanity as opposed to madness. When the kinsmen of Jesus said 'He is beside himself' (ἐξέστη, Mk iii 21), the Syriac has 'He has gone out of his *haunā*.'

Mad'ā (ܡܕܥܐ) is the faculty of *Reason* that distinguishes Man, a faculty that Bardaisan considered distinct from the soul and Divine (Eph. *agst. Bard.* LIX: see Mitchell, II, p. lxxiii).

Re'yānā (ܪܥܝܢܐ) is the commonest Syriac word for *Thought* or Mind.

Maḥshabthā (ܡܚܫܒܬܐ) I render *Imagination*, because it generally seems to contain the notion of something freshly invented. Thus in Mitchell, I, p. lxiii, it is said "sometimes HULE acquired Thought," but I believe that "once upon a time HŪLĒ got a notion" would be a more accurate as well as a more idiomatic English rendering.

Tar'ithā (ܬܪܥܝܬܐ) has generally the notion of *Intention*, the Mind regarded as Will. A good example of its use will be found in Mitchell, II, p. 235.

MANICHAEAN 'EUCHARIST.'

Bread and Fruit being ceremonially offered as food for an 'Elect' Manichee. See pp. 45 f., 56 note². 60.

ܝܘܡ ܡܢ ܝܘܡ ܡܙܥܪ ܙܥܪ
ܡܢܝܢܗܘܢ ܕܢܦܫܬܐ
ܒܕܡܬܛܠܠܢ ܘܣܠܩܢ

Yōm min yōm miz'ar z'ar
minyānhēn dnaphshāthā
badmiṣṭallān wsālḳān . .

"Day by day diminishes
The number of the Souls (below)
As they are distilled and mount up."

II

WE have seen what Mani taught about the *Past*, about the eternal opposition of Light and Dark, how the Dark invaded the Realms of Light, and how thereby our mingled world came into being. We must now go on to explain the Manichee view of the *Present*, *i.e.* of the time since the true knowledge of doctrine and conduct has been given to the world by the great Prophet Mani.

In the past men for the most part lived in ignorance and darkness, but God did not leave himself entirely without witness. In the beginning of the book called *Shābūhragān*, written by Mani for King Shapur, son of Ardashir, he says:

> Wisdom and deeds have always from time to time been brought to mankind by the messengers of God. So in one age they have been brought by the messenger called Buddha to India, in another by Zarādusht to Persia, in another by Jesus to the West. Thereupon this revelation has come down, this prophecy in this last age, through me, Mani, messenger of the God of truth to Babylonia.

This quotation is preserved for us by Al-Biruni[1]: a few scraps from this famous work survive among the Soghdian fragments from Turfan edited by Prof. Müller (II, pp. 16, 17), but unfortunately there is not enough to make much connected sense. The sentence quoted by Biruni, however, is exactly paralleled by a statement in Ephraim (Mitchell, II, p. xcviii), which says that the

[1] Sachau's transl., p. 190.

Manichees "say about Hermes in Egypt, and about Plato among the Greeks, and about Jesus who appeared in Judaea, that 'they are Heralds of that Good One to the world.'"

It is easy to see what these two passages imply. They imply a doctrine of a succession of Prophets of the Truth at divers times and in many countries, men with whose doctrine Mani believed himself to be in essential accord. He, of course, was the last and final mouthpiece of Revelation. Like so many others, he thought of himself as living in the 'last age,' and as being himself the last and fullest Herald of the Light. But it is most important to notice that whereas Hermes[1] and Plato and Buddha, and also Zoroaster, stand more or less on a level with a more or less ethnic and geographical significance, Jesus in Mani's system occupies a peculiar position. He was the last of the series before Mani, but he is more than that. To Mani Jesus was a Divine Being, who appeared on earth but was never born of woman; the Christians believed that Jesus had been really crucified, but that was their carnal error. And further, Jesus was not merely the last of the Prophets before Mani and Mani's immediate predecessor; Mani regarded himself as the apostle of Jesus. All his letters began, says Augustine (*c. Faust.* XIII 4), with 'Mani, Apostle of Jesus Christ,' and this has been confirmed by a frag-

[1] That is, of course, 'Hermes Trismegistus': see Faustus ap. Aug. *c. Faust.* XIII 1.

ment from Turfan[1]. The 'Jesus' revered by Mani has a different nature from the Jesus Christ of orthodox Christian theology, and also from the Jesus of the Four Gospels. But after all Mani does mean the same 'Jesus who appeared in Judaea,' and therefore it seems to me impossible to treat Manichaeism apart from its special relation to the various forms of the Christian Religion.

When we ask what rôle is assigned to 'Jesus' in the Manichee system we are met by several difficulties, partly connected with the comparative scantiness of our information, but still more connected with the difference between the terms and conceptions of Manichaeism on the one hand and orthodox Christianity on the other. Orthodox Christianity more or less starts with the religion of Judaism, of the Old Testament. The primal antithesis is between 'God' and 'His Creatures,' of which the race of Men is the noblest species. The main question in Western Christology was whether, and to what extent, 'Jesus who appeared in Judaea' was to be reckoned as belonging to 'God' or the Creatures. But to Mani the ultimate antithesis was not between God and Man, but between Light and Dark. A Man was not a simple unit, much less an elemental unit, but a particle of Light enclosed in an alien and irredeemable envelope: there is no hope for a Man as such, for he is essentially a fortuitous conglomeration. The hope is that his Light-particles—roughly speaking,

[1] Müller, II ('04), p. 26.

very much what we mean by his 'better self'—may escape at death from the dark prison-house of the body. And 'God' represents also a conception quite different from the 'personal,' transcendent, Jahweh of the Old Testament. As used by the Manichees it seems to mean anything wholly composed of and belonging to the Light-substance. The 'Mother of the Living,' the 'Primal Man,' the 'Messenger,' etc., are little more than manifestations of the energy of the Light. They are not even, properly speaking, eternal, for they seem to come into existence to meet a need, as occasion arises—something like the 'Angel of the LORD' in the early books of the Old Testament.

With this view of 'God' and 'man,' it is no wonder that the Jesus honoured by Mani was regarded as human only in appearance. But also He seems to occupy a peculiar position among the hierarchy of Light. Full as our accounts are of the Manichee cosmogony, no tale of theirs survives which purports to give the story of how He was 'evoked' or called into being. He is 'sent' when His presence is needed, but no explanation is given who He is or how He came to be there. Alone among the heavenly denizens He has a personal name, is in fact a person, as Buddha is, or Hermes, or Mani himself. No doubt this is because Jesus, whatever Mani may have thought about Him, is ultimately a certain Person 'who appeared in Judaea' a little more than two hundred years before Mani began to preach.

As to the manner and fashion of that appearance
Mani does not seem to have been so much of an
innovator as is sometimes supposed, if (as I
believe) his view of the historical Jesus was partly
derived from that of the Marcionites. It is im-
probable that he ever saw a copy of the Four
Gospels, and if his knowledge was derived ex-
clusively from the Epistles of Paul, the Syriac
Diatessaron and the Marcionite Gospel,—possibly
from the Gospel of Peter as well,—I can scarcely
wonder that he was unable to think of our Lord
as a real human being. It is true that Mani did
not believe Him to have been really born: nor
did Marcion. Nor again did he believe that Jesus
was crucified, for he is said to have held that the
Jews crucified some one else by mistake; but this
again is an ancient heresy, as old as the well-
known *Acts of John.* To Mani historical happenings
of such a kind were profoundly distasteful, in very
truth a 'scandal.' But the Manichees believed that
they had in their religion the true "word of the
Cross." To them 'Jesus' meant not only revealed
and visible Light and the ennobling doctrine of
the true destiny of the Divine part of man, but
also man's life and salvation through Divine suffering. Faustus the African Manichee claims that
he and his held the true Christian doctrine, and
that the 'suffering Jesus' is not a Divine Man born
from a human mother and the Holy Spirit, but the
fruit which is man's food, "hanging on every tree,
produced by the energy and power of the air that

makes the earth conceive." And he goes on to say: "Wherefore also our reverence for everything is like that of you Catholic Christians about the Bread and the Cup[1]."

Augustine does not find it difficult to expose the inconsistencies in this Christology. And he asks at the end of a triumphant paragraph why Jesus who was crucified should be identified with the powers of vegetation and also with the Divine Being in the Sun, and not also with the Splenditenens and the Atlas and the Primal Man? But the answer is clear, and it is of great importance, when we are seeking to understand this ancient Religion and not merely, like Augustine, to refute it. The answer is that the Splenditenens and the others are only what the author of the Epistle to the Hebrews calls 'ministering spirits,' evoked by Mani for a special purpose or imported by him from some system or other. But 'Jesus' signified Divine Redemption of man, Divine nourishment for man, accompanied somehow by the almost inconceivable idea of Divine suffering for man— and all this effected by 'Jesus who appeared in Judaea.' These are *Christian* ideas: they render the Manichaean religion as set forth by the African

[1] Faustus ap. Aug. *c. Faust.* xx 2: *necnon et spiritus sancti, qui est maiestas tertia, Aeris hunc omnem ambitum sedem fatemur ac diuersorium ; cuius ex uiribus ac spiritali profusione terram quoque concipientem gignere patibilem Iesum, qui est uita ac salus hominum, omni suspensus ex ligno. quapropter et nobis circa uniuersa et uobis similiter erga panem et calicem par religio est.*

Faustus a form of Christianity, though doubtless an inconsistent and heretical form. Above all, they explain to us how it is that Mani, who denied the birth and the real crucifixion of Jesus, called himself nevertheless Jesus' Apostle, and regarded himself as the Paraclete whom Jesus had foretold.

It is time now to come to the *Present*, in the sense of the Church or Society which Mani set up. But first there is still one feature of Mani's cosmogony which we must consider. It is best given in the Description of Manichaeism in the Acts of Archelaus (c. VIII), which tells us that when Jesus was sent on His message of salvation He contrived a vast mechanism, like a water-wheel with twelve buckets, which takes up the souls of men and the light-particles in their bodies as they die to the Moon, which thus waxes for fifteen days. While in the Moon the souls are somehow purged and purified by the Sun, and then the Moon empties itself of the purged Light, whereby it wanes for another fifteen days. The souls when purged are gathered into the Column of Glory (in Syriac, *Estōn Shubḥā*)[1], which is called according to the Acts of Archelaus the 'Perfect Man.' Epiphanius, who transcribes the passage, turns this into ἀὴρ ὁ τέλειοσ but I venture to think he is wrong, and that the myth has its actual origin in Eph. iv 13, where the Apostle speaks of the final result of Salvation as the formation of a

[1] Mitchell, II 208, ll. 37, 38.

43

Perfect Man (εἰσ ἄνδρα τέλειον). No doubt Mani identified this with the Milky Way.

As I said just now, the Acts of Archelaus speak as if this mechanism was set up by Jesus in His historical appearance, but this is not borne out by any other source, and there can be little doubt that Mani thought of it as coeval with the formation of the Sun and Moon out of the first vintage of Light distilled from the Archons. The historical appearance of Jesus was thought of by Mani as for instruction and revelation only—especially to the one really enlightened Apostle, *viz.* Paul. But what Paul had only hinted at, he, Mani, the Paraclete foretold by Jesus, made clear to his disciples. Mani wrote many books, and the system which he excogitated, fantastic and bizarre as it sounds to our ears, seems to have been taught for centuries by the Manichees, and the Church Order which he instituted was strictly maintained to the end.

This Order is one familiar to us in these days from the Buddhists, but they were not the only society which adopted it in antiquity, and I may say at once that I see no sign that Mani was influenced at all by Buddhism. The Order I mean is the fundamental division of the Manichee believers into Monks and Laymen, or as the Manichees called them the *Elect* and the *Hearers*. The 'Elect' alone was the true Manichee, the 'Hearer' was no more than an adherent, but the renunciations exacted of the Elect were severe, and their numbers were comparatively small. The proportion in numbers is not known, but it probably was similar to what obtains in Buddhist countries. All Manichees were vegetarians, but the Elect abstained from wine, from marriage and from property. They were supposed to live a wandering life, possessing no more than food for a day and clothes for a year[1]. Their obligation not to produce fresh life or to take it was so absolute that it extended to the vegetable kingdom: they might neither sow nor reap, nor even break their bread themselves, "lest they pain the Light which was mixed with it[2]." So they went about, as Indian holy men do, with a disciple who prepared their food for them. "And when they wish to eat bread," we read in the *Acta Archelai* (IX), "they pray first, saying to the bread 'I neither reaped thee, nor winnowed thee, nor ground thee, nor set thee in an oven; it was another did this and brought thee to me, I eat thee innocently.' And when he has said this to himself, he says to the disciple 'I have prayed for thee!'" On the other hand, it was one of the first duties of the mere 'Hearers' to provide food for the 'Elect,' so that in a country where there were any Manichees the Elect were sure not to starve. Women as well as men entered the ranks of the Elect, and Ephraim has a curious passage in which he rebukes their

[1] So Biruni, p. 190, confirmed by a text in Müller, II ('04), p. 33.
[2] Mitchell, I, p. xxx.

'idleness[1].' Poor ladies, there was very little that their religion permitted them to do! It is in any case noteworthy that the pious Deacon of Edessa accuses them of no other peccadilloes[2].

But there was a difference between the inner attitude of the Manichee ascetic and the orthodox Christian monk. The latter, whether hermit or coenobite, had retired from the world with a consciousness of sin and a sense of personal unworthiness. It is not for nothing that 'mourner' is one of the Syriac technical terms for a Christian monk. The Manichee Elect does not appear to have been a 'mourner.' He was indeed fenced about with tabus—'touch not, taste not, handle not,'—but by virtue of his profession he was already Righteous, and he was called *Zaddīķā*, *i.e.* 'the righteous,' by his co-religionists. And though he was forbidden to prepare his food himself, yet a sacramental,

[1] Mitchell, I, p. xciii.
[2] Fortunatus, the African 'presbyter' of the Manichees, succeeded in extracting a left-handed testimonial to the morals of the Manichees from Augustine, who (after some preliminary fencing) said: "As for your habits, those only can fully know them who are your Elect. But you know I was not one of your Elect, but a Hearer, so although I have been present at your Prayers, as you have asked—whether you have any Prayers separately by yourselves, God only knows besides yourselves. I certainly in the Prayers where I was present saw nothing disgraceful done, but only noticed contrary to the Faith which afterwards I have learnt and approved that you make your Prayers facing the Sun." Then he goes on to protest that he doesn't know what the Elect may do at their ceremonies (Aug. *c. Fortunatum*, 3). How ungenerous!

indeed an actual physical benefit accrued to the Universe through his eating it. This came to pass through the particles of Light contained in the food passing into his own pure body, for what greater concentration of the Light-substance can there be upon this earth than the person of an abstinent, righteous, Elect Manichee? Ephraim and other orthodox controversialists make merry over this curious belief, but their own theory of digestion was not much more in harmony with our modern knowledge of the processes of metabolism and the methods by which living tissue is nourished.

Exactly *how* the fully qualified Manichee separates the Light that is mixed in the substances with which he is concerned our documents do not inform us. I doubt very much whether Mani himself had a really consistent theory about it. But it seems, from what Ephraim says[1], that the Manichees believed that even a couple of the highest class of Initiates would suffice for what the world needed.

The Hearers, of course, formed the great bulk of the Manichaean community. They were allowed to marry and hold property, in fact, to live in the world like other folk. Besides these two main classes there were higher orders, about which we know little more than the names, and in any case they were very few in number. At the head of all was a Successor of Mani, who was at first

[1] See Mitchell, II, p. xcviii.

supposed not to quit Babylonia, but this was afterwards modified as the result of persecution[1].

The religious duties of the Manichee Hearers can best be inferred from the *Khuastuanift*, *i.e.* 'Confession,' an important document that has been recovered almost in its entirety from the finds in Chinese Turkestan. Prof. von Le Coq found the beginning in Manichee script at Khotscho near Turfan, Prof. Radloff brought to Petersburg a large fragment in Uïgur script, and Sir Aurel Stein found in the district S.E. of Tunhuang a roll in Manichee script containing almost all except the beginning. The document is in the old Turkestan Turkish language and contains a detailed confession of sins. It has been excellently edited by v. Le Coq in the *Journal of the Royal Asiatic Society* for 1911, pp. 277–314 and again by Prof. W. Bang in *Muséon* for 1923 (vol. XXXVI), pp. 137–242[2].

The document consists of a preamble, followed by a confession of fifteen kinds of sins, each section ending with the Persian (not Turkish) formula *Manāstār ḥirʒa*, which means 'O cleanse

[1] On the various names for the Hierarchy, see the Separate Note (Appendix 1, p. 105).

[2] I quote by von Le Coq's numbered lines (1, 1–39; 1–338). There is a note on the meaning of the word *Khuastuanift* by Prof. Müller in the *Sitzungsberichte* of the Berlin Academy for 1909, p. 1212. But why does he call the Armenian *Khostovanutiun* a borrowed word?

our spots!¹,' the whole ending with a general acknowledgement of sinfulness. But the *Khuastuanift* is more than a mere confession. Each section begins by formulating the true Manichee doctrine, and then goes on to say: "if we, then, have neglected such a practice or denied such a doctrine we are sinful and must cry *Manāstār ḥīrẓa*." It is thus for practical purposes a profession of Faith also, and therefore worthy now of our particular attention. We shall find in it references to the primordial battle between Light and Dark already described, and to the scheme of redemption through the Sun and Moon. But in order to make the main principle on which the *Khuastuanift* is arranged intelligible one or two points of Manichaean nomenclature and theology must be borne in mind.

First of all, it is not easy to express what the Manichees mean when they say 'God,' for to them 'God' is rather a substance than a person, using these contentious words in their modern connotation. *Tängri* in Manichee Turkish is 'God,' *kün* is 'day,' *ai* is 'month.' The last two words mean 'sun' and 'moon' respectively, so that *kün ai tängri* is 'Sun-Moon-God².' This expression occurs in the *Khuastuanift* more than half-a-dozen times, but it is never quite clear whether it means 'the

¹ The actual formula occurs in the Soghdian Persian texts, *e.g.* Müller, II, p. 61. As to the exact meaning, Müller, II 93 gives 'Befleckung' for '*astār*, and on p. 67 *ḥērẓa* is used in a context which speaks of 'dirt' and 'stink.'
² In Turkish there is no word for 'and'!

divine sun and moon' or 'the God of the Sun and Moon': the two expressions coalesce in this Turkish and I doubt whether those who used the *Khuastuanift* distinguished between the two notions. It is the same with *yarūq tängri*: are we to render this 'the Light-God,' or 'the God of the Light,' or 'the divine Light'? I have here chosen to render *tängri* by 'divine' rather than 'God,' because (as we shall see) the Supreme God when thought of as personal is called *Äzrua, i.e.* the Persian *Zrvān*, which corresponds almost exactly with what we mean when we speak of 'the Eternal.'

Similarly the Primal Man is here called *Khormuzta, i.e.* 'Ormuzd,' but this does not seem to imply any mixture with Persian or Magian religion or myth. Most of the other terms explain themselves, such as the *Burkhāns, i.e.* the true Prophets, or are at present inexplicable in detail, such as the exact nature of the *vosanti*-fast (l. 246) or the *yimki*-service (ll. 273 ff.).

But further we have to bear in mind the fourfold nature of God according to Manichee theology. In the words of the *Fihrist*[1]: "Mani enjoined....belief in the Four great things—God, His Light, His Power, His Wisdom. And *God* is the King of the Paradise of Light, His *Light* is the Sun and Moon, His *Power* is the Five Angels, *viz*. the Air, the Wind, the Light, the Water and the Fire, and His *Wisdom* is the Holy Religion,"

[1] Flügel, pp. 64, 95.

which last in the *Khuastuanift* is identified sometimes with the Prophets who announced it, sometimes with the ordinances themselves. In any case this four-fold conception of the Divine determines a good deal of the structure of our document.

With these preliminaries we can come to the *Khuastuanift* itself. The Prologue sets forth that as the Divine Khormuzta with the Divine Five came down from heaven to battle against the forces of the Demons of Darkness, but was overcome and became temporarily separated from the eternal dwelling of the Gods and lost his Divine Light, so we the penitent Manichees, if we have erred and lost touch with Azrua the pure bright God and have become intermingled with the Dark [may nevertheless hope to be restored even as the Primal Man was][1].

§ 1. *Blasphemy against God.* The 'blasphemies' mentioned are that God has made all things, both what is Good and what is Bad; that Khormuzta and the Demon of Darkness are brothers (*i.e.* both created by the Good God)[2]; that it is He, Azrua, who creates the eternal Gods, that it is God who produces or destroys individual life. "My God! in trespass unwittingly to God these great blasphemy words should we have spoken, my God!

[1] Here is a short lacuna in the text.
[2] This was regarded by the Manichees as a Zoroastrian heresy: "They pray to the burning Fire, and they confess themselves that their end will be in Fire. And they say that Ormuzd and Ahriman are brothers..." This important fragment is printed in Müller, II (1904), p. 95.

now I, Raimast Färzind, I repent, I pray, from sin escaping, *Manāstār ḫirẓa!*"

It would be difficult, I think, to express in fewer sentences the essential paradoxes of Manichee theology. It should be noted, in view of § 8, that this first part of the *Khuastuanift* is meant to refer to sins committed before conversion or coming to a knowledge of the truth.

§ 2. *Blasphemy against Sun and Moon.* The true purpose of the divine Sun and Moon is to purify the Light recovered from the earth. If then, says our document, we have dared to say that Sun and Moon are dead[1], that their rising and setting are mechanical (*lit.* 'powerless'), and that our bodies existed before the Sun and Moon, for this unwitting sin we pray *Manāstār ḫirẓa!*

This sounds almost as if the local alternative to Manichaean belief was the naïve idea that each day sees a new Sun and each month a new Moon, —like Horace's *Nouaeque pergunt* INTERIRE *lunae.*

§ 3. *Blasphemy against and injury to the Divine Five.* The Five divine Elements, Air, Wind, Light, Water, Fire, which formed the panoply of the Primal Man (here called 'Khormuzta')[2], having

---

[1] *Sic.* The words are *kün ai ölür*, without *tngri* ('divine'): so omit 'the God of' from v. Le Coq's trans., l. 23.

[2] Prof. v. Le Coq's translation here requires revision. *Khormuẓta* (='Ormuzd') corresponds to *'Ōḥarmīẓd bē* in Müller, II 20, where the parallel in the *Fihrist* makes it quite clear that in Manichee nomenclature 'Ormuzd' is used for the Primal Man, not for the eternal 'Father of Greatness,' who is called *Bai Zrvān* in the Persian, and

been intermingled with the Dark in battling against Sin and Demonry, were unable to return to heaven and are now upon this earth, where they give radiancy and light and consistency to the things it produces: if then, say the Manichees, we have in any way harmed these divine Elements, "if with the ten snake-headed finger-ends and the thirty-two teeth by taking living beings for food and drink we should ever have pained God, and so sinned against the dry or wet earth, the five kinds of animals, or the five kinds of trees, then now, my God, escaping sin we cry *Manāstār ḥirẓa!*"

§ 4. *Offences against the Prophets and the Elect.* The fourth section corresponds to God's Wisdom, *i.e.* the true Manichaean religion as revealed by the Burkhāns, or Prophets, culminating in Mani. If then they have done anything against the Burkhāns in the past or the pure Elect in the present, or if having accepted God's Law[1], they should have broken it by not spreading it, then they say *Manāstār ḥirẓa!*

§ 5. *Offences against animals, including Man.* The five kinds of animals are Man, Quadrupeds, Flying animals, Water animals, and (lowest of all) Things that creep on the earth: "my God, these five kinds....should we ever have frightened or

Aẓrua in the Turkish texts. Prof. Bang (p. 172 ff.) further has proved that *Khormuẓta oghlani* means 'Ormuzd's brood' or 'Ormuzd's troop,' not 'Ormuzd's sons.'

[1] *Nom*, a word said to be ultimately derived from νόμοσ, *i.e.* the Manichee Religion.

scared, beaten or struck, angered or pained them, or killed them"—then we must say *Manāstār ḥīrẓa!* § 6. *Social offences.* The ten offences enumerated are: Falsehood, perjury, testifying for a wicked man, persecuting an innocent man, inducing enmity by tale-bearing, sorcery, killing many animals, fraud, untrustworthiness in deposits (?), deeds displeasing to the Sun and Moon, either before or after the reciters became True Believers. § 7. *Wrong religious observances done through ignorance.* A man who adheres to a false Religion or worships the Demon by the name of God is at the entrance of the two poison-laden roads that lead to Hell. If therefore the reciters of the *Khuastuanift* have believed in the wrong Prophets, or have fasted the wrong fasts, or given the wrong alms, or tried to acquire merit by doing the wrong deeds, or have killed living animals in sacrifice, then—*Manāstār ḥīrẓa!* § 8. *Offences committed after entering Religion.* The preamble to this section is worth giving in full, as it forms a sort of short Manichaean *Credo*[1].

[1] The two terms *tngri yir* and *yir tngri* must surely be distinguished. *Tngri yir* means 'divine land,' 'the Paradise of God,' as Prof. v. Le Coq translates it (l. 160). But *yir tngri* is here used for the visible 'earth and heaven,' *i.e.* land and sky. The use of the term is clear from the Colophon edited in *Türkische Manichaica* III (1922), p. 34, ll. 10, 11. *Arqon yir tngri* (l. 169), therefore, should mean the Archon's land and sky, *i.e.* the Demonic elements in the visible universe. This way of analysing the phrase explains how ἄρχων and *tängri* can be used together, which v. Le Coq notes as strange (p. 303). But it must be noted that Prof. Bang

Since coming to know the True God and the Pure Law, we have learned the Law of the Two Roots and the Three Moments, that the Light-root is God-land, the Dark-root is Hell-land; yea, we learned what had been in existence before land and sky existed, why God and Demon had battled against each other, how Light and Dark had intermingled, and who had created land and sky; yea, we learned in what way this land and sky will be annihilated, and how Light and Dark will be separated, and what will happen afterwards: to the divine Azrua, the divine Sun and Moon, the divine Power, and the Burkhans we turned, we trusted, we became Hearers (*i.e.* Manichees). Four bright Seals on our hearts have we sealed, (1) To Love, the seal of the divine Azrua, (2) To Believe, the seal of the divine Sun and Moon, (3) To Fear, the seal of the Five divine elements[1], (4) Wise Wisdom, the seal of the Burkhans.

Such is the Manichee *Credo*, which as will have been seen is permeated by the four-fold conception of God to which I referred above. The section goes on in the usual way to declare that should the penitents have in any way deserted or violated their faith, then they beg for restitution by the usual formula[2].

has given reasons for thinking that *arqon* here is a Turkish word, *lit.* 'backwards' and so used for 'ultimately.'

[1] Note how the divine Power (*lit.* 'powerful God') is identical with the divine Five.

[2] A perfectly literal translation of this section of the *Khuastuanift*, retaining as far as possible the Turkish idiom, may be of interest.

"8th. True God, pure Law, since our coming to know... Two-Roots, Three-Moments Law we knew...Light Root God-Land, Dark Root Hell-Land we knew...yea, Land-Heaven when not, what to say there was we knew... God, Demon, why having battled...Light, Dark, how intermingled, Earth-Heaven, who to say had created we knew...yea, *arqon* Earth-Heaven, why it will become

§ 9. *The Ten Commandments.* These are described as to be kept "three with the mouth, three with the heart, three with the hand, and one with the whole self." If through bad companions or through attachment to material things these have been broken, then they say *Manāstār hīrza!*[1]

§ 10. *Remissness in worship.* Four benedictions with one mind and heart should be said every day upon Azrua, the Sun and Moon, the Powerful God and upon the Burkhans: should these benedictions through our carelessness have failed to reach their destination, then—*Manāstār hīrza!*

§ 11. *Remissness in alms.* Seven kinds of alms should be given as a religious duty out of what Heaven has prospered us[2]. If then we have stinted our alms, or have given food that should have been reserved for the Elect to our household or to wicked men or to evil animals, or have thrown it away, thus sending the divine Light to the Evil Place, then—*Manāstār hīrza!*

nothing...Light, Dark, how they will be parted...after this what to say will be we knew...To Azrua-God, to Sun-Moon-God, to Powerful God, to the Burkhans we turned, we trusted, 'Hearers' we became...Four Light-Seals in our heart we sealed, 1st, To Love, Azrua-God's seal; 2nd, To Believe, Sun-Moon-God's seal; 3rd, To Fear, Five-God's seal; 4th, Wise Wisdom, the Burkhans' seal."

[1] On the 'Ten Commandments,' see below, p. 60.

[2] This is a guess at the general sense. The text speaks of 'angels' and divine 'callers' and 'answerers,' who give us light that ought to go to God for purification. This seems to mean grain and fruit that ought to go to be eaten by the Elect Ones.

§ 12. *Remissness in fasting.* Fifty days *vosanti-*fast should be kept every year: if we have broken this fast, or not fasted according to Law and Ritual, then—*Manāstār ḥīrẓa!*

§ 13. *Remissness in penitence.* We should confess to God, to the Law and to the Elect every day of the Moon-God (*i.e.* every Monday). If we have been remiss, then—*Manāstār ḥīrẓa!*

§ 14. *Remissness in other religious duties.* Every year we should keep seven *yimḳi*-services and one month's Commandments (*chakḥshapat*). Here again if we have been remiss—*Manāstār ḥīrẓa!*

§ 15. "Every day how many evil thoughts do we think! how many wretched words that should not be spoken do we speak! how many deeds that ought not to be done do we do! With evil deeds, with wretched acts our own selves do we torment! Yea, daily in what we have eaten, the Five-God's Light, through our own selves, our souls, having walked in the love of the insatiable shameless Envy-Demon, goes to the Evil Place. Because of this, my God! from sin escaping we pray *Manāstār ḥīrẓa!*"

My God! imperfect, sinful are we!
Tormentors, twisters are we!
For the insatiable, shameless Envy-Demon's sake,
    by thought, by word, by deed,
    yea, by eyes seeing, by ears hearing, by tongue speaking,
        by hands touching, by legs walking,
    long, endlessly do we pain the Five-God's light, the
        dry-wet Earth, the Five kinds living beings, the
        Five kinds trees plants,

Yea, imperfect, sinful are we!

For the Ten Commandments', the Seven Alms', the Three
  Seals' sake the Hearers' name we hold,
  by deed to do we cannot!

Yea, the Light-Gods, the Pure Law, the God-like Ex-
  pounders, the pure Elect Ones, whenever we should
  have offended, should have accused of error,

Yea, by God's decree in word, in meaning, should we not
  have walked,
  the heart of the Gods should we have twisted,

Yea, the *Yimki*-observance, fasting, benediction, command-
  ment, in Law, in Ritual, whenever we should have
  been unable to keep, whenever we should have been
  wanting, unavailing,
  every day, every month, trespass, sin do we commit!

To the Light-Gods, to the Law's Majesty, to the pure Elect
  Ones, from trespass, from sin escaping, we pray
  Manāstār ḥīrẓa!

This is the conclusion of the *Khuastuanift*
(ll. 308–338). Most of the allusions are clear
enough, from other Manichaean documents or
from earlier passages in the *Khuastuanift* itself. The
'Five-God' is, of course, the remains of the Five
pure elements mixed with the demonic substance
which were absorbed when they were swallowed
by the Archons. Anything that was identifiable
with these pure elements the Manichee held in
reverence, and anything that would free them
from their imprisonment in 'dark' matter it was
his duty to do. Equally, it was his duty not to
do anything that tended still further to imprison
these elements. Naturally, therefore, it was his
duty not to pain these elements by killing the
'five kinds' of animals, and we have seen from

ll. 80–84 of the *Khuastuanift* that the five kinds
were Men, quadrupeds, animals that fly in the air,
animals that live in the water, and lastly those that
creep on the earth[1]. In Section 3 (ll. 42–57) it is
said that the heavens and the earths all exist on
account of the Five-God, and that of everything
on earth the beauty, soul, strength, light, foundation and root is the Five-God. Therefore the
Manichee must not frighten, scare, beat, strike,
anger or pain living beings (ll. 87–93), much less
kill them. How kind, how 'humane'! But further
on in the *Khuastuanift*, in the eleventh section, we
find that this kindness is purely negative, and that
the Manichee Hearers must not do good unto all
men or to beasts if it in any way interferes with
the sacred duty of feeding the household of faith,
i.e. the Elect *Zaddīks*. So if they have stinted
giving alms, or have been unable to give the
Seven legal kinds of Alms perfectly, which ought
to have gone to God for purification, and instead
have given it to their house and household, or to
men inclined to evil deeds, or to bad living and
moving creatures (*e.g.* I suppose, to dogs), and so
the Light has been spilled or dispersed,—then it
seems that they had no other resource but to recite
their *Khuastuanift* and to say *Manāstār hīrza!*

That is why Augustine can declare to Faustus
(vi 25) that the Manichees break the Sixth Com-
mandment, though they profess never to take

[1] Prof. v. Le Coq (p. 302) notes that Augustine knows
of exactly the same division of animals.

life: "fearing lest a member of your God should be bound in flesh," he says, "you do not give bread to the hungry. From fear of a fancied homicide you commit a real one. So when you come across a hungry man, who may die if you do not give him food, you are certain to be reckoned a murderer, either by the Law of God if you don't give, or by the Law of Mani if you do!" Perhaps Augustine is not quite fair[1]: he is certainly unsympathetic. But his criticism is concerned with a real difference between Christian and Manichee ethics. It can be expressed in a single sentence: Christianity is concerned with persons, Manichaeism with things. Christian sympathy goes out to men and women, who are even in a fallen state regarded as in the image of God and for whom Christ has died, and this sympathy has been in modern times, by a natural transition, extended to other animals. The sympathy of the Manichee was directed not towards men, but towards the Light imprisoned in men. Men were, to some extent, and at second hand, in the image of God, but they were only a sort of pirated copy, made by the evil, dark Archons to imitate the Messenger of the Light who had appeared to them.

The Ten Commandments which Manichee

---

[1] As Flügel remarks (p. 300), Augustine admits in *De Moribus Manichaeorum*, ii 16, that Manichees were willing to give *money* to the needy. It was Bread and Fruits and Water that should only be given to the Elect.

Hearers had to keep are enumerated for us by
Shahrastani and in the *Fihrist* (Flügel, p. 95 f.).
They are to avoid (1) Idolatry, (2) Lying, (3)
Greed, (4) Killing, (5) Adultery, (6) Theft, (7) In-
cantations and Magic, (8) Holding two opinions,
i.e. Doubts about Religion, (9) Slackness and
Negligence in Business, and (10) they are to pray
four (or seven) times in the day. Shahrastani gives
the same list except that for (8) and (9) he sub-
stitutes giving a Tenth in alms and keeping the
Truth. Probably the latter means Manichaean
orthodoxy and so is equivalent to (8), and the
former is really equivalent to (9), for the more
industrious a man is the more he will have to
tithe. In the *Khuastuanift* the Commandments are not
enumerated, but it is said that three are to be kept
with the mouth, three with the heart, three with the
hand, and one (doubtless the last) with the whole self.

But the special value of the *Khuastuanift* lies
not so much in the elucidation of particular details
of the Manichee Religion as the view that it gives
us of that Religion as a whole, as a working system,
apart from polemics. Prof. Alfaric has given a
fair résumé in his *Écritures Manichéennes* (II 134-5):
if mine differs a little from his, it is because I
venture to think the arrangement actually given
is a little more 'rigoureux' than he supposes.
M. Alfaric (p. 135) regards God as thought of by
Manichees under the form of a Trinity, but really
they thought of God as a Quaternity, and we have
seen that the Four-fold conception of God—God,

His Light, His Power, His revealed Wisdom—
recurs again and again, and has a determining effect
upon the very structure of the *Khuastuanift*.

What are we to think about it as a scheme of
life? Of course, we must not be too much prejudiced against the Manichee Religion on account
of its fantastic astronomy. Again, any confession
of sins, real or hypothetical, makes rather melancholy reading: it is a pathological document, a
record of ill-health, actual or hypothetical. Moreover, most religious formularies are somewhat
one-sided and do not depict the whole balance of
the religion with which they are concerned. The
Christian Creeds, for instance, are admirable
documents in their way, but they do not present
a life-like portrait of the Christian Religion as
a whole: they leave out Christian conduct and
devotion and Christian worship. The *Khuastuanift*
is in this respect more complete. It begins with
theology, but it goes on to deal with social duties
and ritual obligations. Of the several sections,
five deal with doctrine and six with ritual. It is
obvious at the first glance that Mani's is an austere
religion, and like all ancient systems a great deal
of importance is laid on correct ritual. It is therefore remarkable that three whole sections (§§ 5, 6
and 9) are concerned with social duties, for I
count the distribution of alms in § 11 as a ritual
rather than as a social act. It is indeed 'a fugitive
and cloistered virtue,' much more concerned with
the avoidance of harm than the contrivance of

good, but therein it corresponds only too closely to a great deal of traditional Christian ethics. And before we judge the Manichaean system too harshly notice should be taken of the tone of real emotion that runs through the final General Confession.

What does not appear quite clearly from this text, or from any other Manichaean document, so far as I know, is the nature of the forgiveness asked for. The penitent Christian, who is dealing with a personal God, is grieved to lose God's favour, he is sorry that he has made God sorry. Perhaps this is what is meant in the *Khuastuanift* (ll. 51, 329) by "twisting the heart of the Gods." Yet even so, in the Manichee system this is chiefly done by harming, that is to say, mixing water, fire, light, wind, with the dirty earth. A tardy European legislation has made some progress with the prevention of the pollution of rivers: this has been done for the benefit of Men who drink the water or (in some cases) of Fish that live in it. In a Manichee state such legislation might conceivably have been undertaken, but it would have been for the sake of the Water itself, in order that it might more easily evaporate altogether and be lost to this world!

In § 8 of the *Khuastuanift* the Manichees declare that they have learned how in the end Light and Dark will be finally and completely separated, and also that they know what will happen afterwards. It is time to finish this Lecture, now that we have considered the Manichee doctrine about the *Past* and the *Present*, by glancing at their doctrine about the *Future*.

Schemes of eschatology, anticipations of the End of all things, are liable to change from time to time, like the unsubstantial pictures in the clouds of heaven. But the Manichee doctrine seems to have been singularly stable. Its main features are simple enough. The Manichees, like the Christians, looked forward to a victorious end of the present state of things. When all the Light has been distilled and separated from the base material, then Evil, which is the result of the mixture of the Light and the Dark, will have disappeared. The 'Earth of Light' in which God dwells and which is itself Divine will be complete and inviolate, and the powers of the Dark will be confined within their own original domain, round which the Heavenly Builder, whom the Syriac-speaking Manichees called the great Bān, will have built a wall and fence, so that it will be the Grave of the Darkness for ever[1].

Two points must here be noted in conclusion. We read in the *Fihrist* (p. 90) that after all the particles of Light that the Sun and Moon can distil have been extracted from the earth, the earth itself will be set on fire and it will burn until all the heavenly material has been refined out from it: this great final Bonfire will last 1468 years. No satisfactory explanation of this curious number

[1] See *e.g.* Mitchell, I, pp. xxx, xlvii, lxxv.

has been found, but among the fragments of the eschatological work published by Prof. Müller (II, pp. 11–25), which is either a Soghdian translation of Mani's *Shābūhragān*, or a work which contains extensive extracts from it, we find on one leaf the Great Fire is spoken of, and its duration is there given as 1468 years. I mention this point to illustrate the stability of the Manichaean doctrine of the future, because it gives us some right to lay stress on the point that follows.

Evodius, the friend and correspondent of S. Augustine, tells us (*De Fid. c. Manich.* 5) that the Manichees taught in the *Epistula Fundamenti* that the Souls which deliberately preferred Darkness to Light and the sensual life to redemption will remain for ever conjoined with matter in the region of the Dark. Such souls, together with the rest of the Dark substance from which all the Light has been extracted, will be compacted together in a great round Clod (*globus*). Titus of Bostra tells us the same[1], and the same doctrine is set forth in the *Acta Archelai* x, the original Greek of which, as quoted by Epiphanius, 646, speaks of the evil man as being for ever δεδεμένοσ εἰσ τὴν βῶλον. In agreement with all this we read at the end of Ephraim's Third Discourse to Hypatius:

[1] Tit. Bostr. A 41: the sinful souls...ἐν τῇ βώλῳ ἐμπαγήσασθαι ἅμα τῇ κακίᾳ λέγων. The wicked Soul is thus turned into a literal villain, *ascriptus glebae*.

How do they say that some of those Souls who have sinned much and have been guilty of great unbelief, those which are found like dregs in the midst of that which they call BOLOS,—as they say, that "when the Fire dissolves all, within it (*i.e.* the Bolus) is collected everything that is mixed and mingled in created things from the Lights," and "those Souls who have done much wickedness are assigned to the dominion of the Darkness when it is tormented[1]."

It will be remembered that Ephraim is writing in Syriac, and the Manichaean documents with which he is concerned are not translations from the Greek but Syriac originals. Yet he introduces BOLOS (ܒܘܠܘܣ) as a Manichaean technical term.

I venture to think it is clear from all these testimonies that Mani not only held this doctrine and gave it a place in one of his principal works, the Πραγματεία or "Great Epistle to Patticius," but that he called this mass of burning filth the BOLOS, a word which is not Syriac at all, but the Greek word for 'a clod[2].'

Alexander of Lycopolis, himself a heathen, treats Manichaeism as a New Christianity. This view of it has been unpopular in recent years, for modern scholars have preferred to see in it a more or less independent Oriental Religion, and have

[1] Mitchell, I, p. 87 f.: the translation I, p. lxxii, must be corrected by vol. II, pp. cxxxix and 236.

[2] So little is ܒܘܠܘܣ a Syriac word that the ancient Syriac version of Titus of Bostra, not used by Ephraim but certainly made before 411 A.D., transliterates it in the form *bōlārā* (*Tit. Bost. Syriace*, 31[16]).

tended to consider the form of it which spread to the West, and to which Augustine was for so many years a convert, as an adaptation fitted to a land where Catholic Christianity had become the established religion. But the name of the *Bolus*, now attested in the Syriac of Ephraim, cannot have come from anything but a Greek source. It suggests to us that Mani drew his inspiration from the West, as much as, if not more than, from the East around him.

"MANI, NEW FULL-MOON!"

See p. 93

"In seeking a doctrine of the Fall...no view will be found adequate which regards the fall of man as something which took place in this world under our present conditions of being."

Canon PETER GREEN, *The Problem of Evil*, p. 131.

III

WE have now passed in survey the outline of the Religion of Mani, what he taught about the two eternal principles of Light and Dark, and about the Past, the Present and the Future. Where did he get it from? From what sources did he derive his ideas? Ought Manichaeism to be classed as an independent religion or as a Christian heresy?

Of course in one sense it does not matter. The followers of Mani will not in any case be included in schemes for the reunion of Christendom, because there are none. But there is an interest in tracing the affiliation of ideas, and the better we understand in what way and from what quarter Mani came by those that he so attractively put forward to his contemporaries sixteen centuries ago, the more real and living his system will be to us to-day.

Obviously Manichaeism is a synthesis, a construction, made of diverse materials. It owed its success to its attractiveness, for it offered no other credentials. No outstanding miracle was worked in Mani's favour, and from the beginning it was persecuted by the civil and religious authorities of the civilized world. It is a wonder that it took root at all, and again that it did not wither away after Mani's execution. Dr Gillis Wetter is no doubt right in laying stress upon the personality of Mani himself, the Prophet of his own new Religion. Unfortunately he no longer stands

71

before our eyes as a living man. In the newly-found fragments from Turkestan he has been sublimated into a sort of Divine Avatar, and the Christian accounts such as the Acts of Archelaus are too fabulous and spiteful to be of any use to us[1].

Both the two main theories about the general origin of Mani's system have had supporters in ancient times. Most Christian documents, from Mark the Deacon onwards, treat Manichaeism as in the main a Christian heresy, while Eznik of Kolb, the Armenian writer of the 5th century, writing against Zoroastrianism, treats Manichaeism as a variety of Persian religion. But he does not go into it very deeply, and only brings it forward as another religion, found in Persian lands, which is Dualistic in character, which nevertheless the Persians persecuted[2].

Mani, before he began his wandering career, lived in Seleucia-Ctesiphon, then the great centre of population in Babylonia. In documents written long afterwards, in Turkestan, far away to the north-east, he is called 'Mani from Babel[3],' but this only means from Lower Mesopotamia, or (as we should now say) from 'Irāq. The old city of Babylon had already become deserted and was crumbling away, and with it had crumbled away the old religion of 'Chaldea' and the knowledge of

[1] For the unhistorical and untrustworthy nature of the narrative of the *Acta Archelai* see especially Flügel, pp. 4–30.
[2] *Eznik* (Schmid's translation), p. 94 f.
[3] Müller, II 51.

the cuneiform script. Chaldaism had come to mean little more than Astrology. Seleucia, on the other hand, had been a Greek or semi-Greek city. With the coming of the Sasanians, when Mani was a little boy, Persian influence had no doubt greatly increased, but the ordinary language spoken was Aramaic, not Persian: this may safely be inferred from the fact that the language of the Mandaean religion, which is a local religion, at least in the form we know it, is Aramaic. Mani did not write in this dialect, so far as we know, but in an Aramaic that was far more like 'classical' Syriac, the dialect of Edessa. He used a peculiar script, and his followers used the same for centuries, so that every scrap of a Manichaean document can be recognized as such, even if too small or mutilated to yield a continuous sense. All the Soghdian documents from Turkestan and a good many of the Turkish ones are written in this script. It is therefore important to notice that the tiny bits of 'Manichaean' writing that have turned up in the West are all in the Syriac language, not in Mandaean or Palmyrene or some other Aramaic dialect[1].

Now Seleucia-Ctesiphon was a great mart, a meeting-place of East and West, in which the Eastern influence was mainly Persian, while the

---

[1] The largest bits are the vellum fragment published by Crum (*J.R.A.S.* for 1919, p. 207) and the papyrus fragments from Oxyrhynchus published by Margoliouth (*J. Egyptian Arch.* for 1915, p. 214). See Appendix III.

Western element since the decay of Greek-speaking civilization in Mesopotamia was Syriac. To us Syriac is so 'oriental' a language, that it requires a certain effort of mind to remember that to an inhabitant of Babylonia the chief seats of Aramaic civilization lay to the West, in the direction of the Roman Empire. Greek influence, if we are about to find it in Manichaeism, will have come to Mani through a Syriac channel.

"Mani," says the *Fihrist*, "composed seven books, one in Persian and six in Syriac[1]." Of these one, the *Shābūhragān*, was composed for the benefit of King Shapur: no doubt that is the one composed in Persian, and the circumstances of its composition explain why it was not in Syriac. Otherwise Mani wrote in Syriac; it is as a Syriac-speaking, Syriac-writing personage that he comes before us, so that the natural source of his inherited or acquired ideas would be that which was current in the Syriac literature of his time. Now of the early writers who are concerned with Mani only one is a native Mesopotamian, writing in Syriac himself with a knowledge of the mental atmosphere of the Syriac-speaking world. This is S. Ephraim, who wrote at Edessa and died there in 373, but who was born still further to the east in Nisibis. We turn therefore to Ephraim and find a quite definite thesis as to the origin of Mani's conceptions: according to Ephraim Mani's system is a fantastic reproduction of the heretical Christian

[1] Flügel, p. 102.

philosopher Bardaiṣān and the heretical Christian churchman Marcion.

I believe that, in the main, S. Ephraim is right. But before going on to explain the ideas of Bardaisan and Marcion there is one preliminary objection to be considered. Christianity, it may be said, is monotheistic; Mani's system is dualistic. Persian religion, the religion of Zoroaster, is the very type of dualistic religion: does not this at once stamp Manichaeism, which had its rise within the domains of the Sasanian Empire, on the very borders of Persia, as a mere variant of Zoroastrianism?

The answer is that dualism is not confined to the religion of Zoroaster. It is a tendency, a view of the world, found among many who would disclaim altogether the name of dualist. There are, of course, certain things that an orthodox Christian must not say. He must say that God created all things, both men and angels, including Satan. But in practice Satan was believed in as an independent power, who won victories among men against the will of God, and was destined to exist for ever in the company of those souls whom he had dragged down to Hell. God created Satan good, no doubt, and afterwards Satan rebelled. But who created the impulse which led Satan to rebel? Was it eternally there? I am not going now to discuss these questions, but it is obvious that the old-fashioned religious view of the Devil is not so very different from the 'dualism' of Mani.

To come back to Ephraim, we shall see that Marcion and Bardaisan were both as dualistic as Mani, and neither of these, especially Marcion, can be accused of deriving his ideas from Persia. Bardaiṣān, or, as the Greeks called him, Bardesanes, was known in his own country of Edessa as 'the Aramaean Philosopher[1].' He was born in 154 and must have become converted to Christianity soon after it came to Edessa. He was a friend of Abgar IX, the last real King of Edessa, and was a man apparently of wealth and certainly of culture. He enjoyed a great reputation as an astronomer, and one of his immediate disciples wrote a book, a sort of Platonic Dialogue, on *Fate*, in which Bardaisan himself is the chief speaker and which no doubt reflects his teaching. The Church decided that Bardaisan was a heretic, but his heresy is not very apparent in the Dialogue, and to understand in what it consisted we must go to a later writer, Moses bar Kepha[2], whose statements, however, are borne out by the less systematic, but much more ancient, evidence of Ephraim.

Moses bar Kepha says:

Bardaisan held about this world that it is composed of Five Entities or primordial Elements (*īthyē*), *viz.*, Fire and Wind and Water and Light and Darkness. Each of these was standing in its own region, Light in the East, Wind

[1] Mitchell, ii, pp. iii, cvi.

[2] The account of Bardaisan's doctrines which here follows is taken from my Introductory Essay prefixed to the Second Volume of Mitchell's book, pp. cxxii–cxxxi.

in the West, Fire in the South, Water in the North, the Lord of them all in the Height, and their Enemy the Dark in the Depth below. Once upon a time, whether from some external body or by chance, they were hurled one against the other, and the Dark ventured to come up from the Depth to mingle together with them. Then the pure Entities began to try and keep away from the Dark and appealed to the mercy of the Most High to deliver them from the dirty colour that was being mingled with them, *i.e.* from the Dark. Then, says he, at the sound of the commotion the Word of the Intention of the Most High, which is the Messiah, came down and cut off the Dark from being in the midst of the pure Elements, and it was hurled down, and He set up the pure Elements again in their places in their symbolic cruciform order. As for that mixture which came into being from the Elements and the Dark their enemy, He constituted from it this World and set it in the midst, that no further mixture might be made, while it is being cleansed by conception and birth till it is perfect.

Exactly what is meant by the last sentence is obscure. Bardaisan regarded man as naturally mortal and held that only the immortal soul is redeemed by Christ. But unlike Mani and Marcion he was not an ascetic. He was himself a married man, and did not regard generation and birth with abhorrence as a further enmeshing of the Divine substance in matter. On the contrary, he seems to have believed that souls at death who kept the word of Jesus did not taste death, but crossed over into the 'bridal-chamber of Light[1]'; and as fresh generations of men come on, also all containing Souls similar to those which had attained the region of Light, it must have seemed to Bar-

---

[1] See Mitchell, II, p. lxxvii.

daisan that they had derived their substance from the primordial Mixture. Conception and birth, therefore, is the process by which something is produced which has the chance of escaping from this mixed world and rejoining the pure region of Light.

This final deduction is the very antithesis of Mani's, but the premises are very much alike. Bardaisan taught that God and the uncreated eternal Elements, including the harmful Dark, existed in Space in a happy state of equilibrium before our World came into being; then something occurred to disturb this equilibrium, whereby general disaster was threatened, but God came to the rescue and confined within certain limits the damage already done and provided for its eventual reparation.

All this corresponds in a sense to the ordinary Christian doctrine of the 'Fall,' but it differs from it inasmuch as it puts the Fall before the construction of our World—nay more, it makes the Fall to be the cause of this World, not a regrettable incident occurring after this World had been made. In this the Bardesanian doctrine agrees with the doctrine of Mani, and I venture to think that S. Ephraim is right when he regards the main principle of the cosmogony of Mani as derived from Bardaisan[1]. A further resemblance between Bardaisan and Mani is afforded by the fact that both regard the evil Element as Darkness, or rather the Dark Substance.

[1] See Mitchell, I, pp. xc and xcix.

But Mani and Bardaisan are very different in their mental outlook. In the 'Refutations' of Ephraim, as also in the Dialogue on Fate, Bardaisan appears as a matter-of-fact man of science. To us, no doubt, it is science falsely so called, speculations as groundless as his derivations of the names of the Aramaic Months. But such as it is, it is positive doctrine about matter and sense-perception; there is no parabolic setting forth of the ways of Divine redemption. Light is light, Fire is fire, not a part or aspect of God. Bardaisan's cosmology is a conflict of forces, Mani's is a drama enacted by a crowd of supernatural persons. When the fatal Mixture has been made, he is not content until he has excogitated a set of Angels to attend to it, the *Splenditenens* to suspend it, the *Atlas* to bear it up, the *Adamas* to defend it with spear and shield. Sun and Moon and the Sun-Moon-God are hardly distinguished. In Bardaisan we see the double influence that has led to monotheism, the influence of the religion of the Old Testament on the one hand, which is so jealous of allowing the name of God to any but the One ultimate Ruler, and on the other the influence of Greek Philosophy that from its very beginnings in Thales and Heraclitus has tended to take away the constitution of things from the personal Gods of Olympus and find it in some Element or combination of Elements.

But if Mani derived his science from Bardaisan he went elsewhere for his moral and social teaching. Ephraim's Refutations go far to shew that here Mani's master was Marcion. Fifty years ago Marcion was treated as one of the Gnostics, and we are only beginning to realize that he was not one of any company, but a great and original religious genius, the most remarkable Christian of the 2nd century. Moreover he founded not a mere school, but a Church, an organization so well arranged that notwithstanding almost continual persecution it was almost as long-lived as that of Mani. Certainly we see from the numerous polemical references, and now from Ephraim's three elaborate Refutations, that the Marcionites were a real force among the Christians of Meso-potamia, at least till the 5th century.

The essential fact about Marcion is that he was a Christian Dissenter. Other heretics were heretics, because they were only half-Christian, but Marcion's religion was essentially Christian and Biblical. He was a Dissenter from the orthodox interpretation of the Bible, but his philosophy starts from it. And as I understand him, Marcion, unlike Bardaisan and Mani, was only a cosmologist by accident, he was essentially concerned with morals and the working of the mind and what may be called the psychology of forgiveness.

He taught a rather clumsy presentation of the Universe as consisting of three Regions, one 'above' the other. In the highest dwelt the Kind Stranger, *le Bon Dieu*; in the lowest, on the earth, was the domain of Matter; between them, above the earth, was the domain of the Creator or Maker, the God of Justice and Law, who had made Man out of Matter in his own image. I have ventured elsewhere[1] to suggest that Marcion would have made his meaning clearer to us in these days if he had spoken of his Kind Stranger as being in a 'fourth dimension,' for the essential thing about this Stranger who can and will forgive freely is that He is not in or of this tangible and measurable world. At least this is so, except in so far as the very notions in Marcion's mind are part of the whole of Nature. With this proviso, the whole of Marcion's system is essentially built upon the same lines as the religion outlined in Huxley's famous Romanes Lecture. Nature is red in tooth and claw, in this world an eye is exacted for an eye and a tooth for a tooth (or its equivalent). Action and reaction are equal and opposite, and the Law of the Conservation of Energy seems to be unbroken. But Man can imagine, more or less, another world where it is not the case, and his mind can take refuge in this fairy-land, which is outside the visible universe.

Marcion, as a matter of fact, was one-sided and inconsistent, and orthodox writers were able to shew that even the portions of the Christian tradition that he retained contained much that did not square with his views. But they did less than justice to Marcion's theory of Religion. After all, the Gospel was in some sense new, and it is not

[1] See Mitchell, II, p. cxxi.

altogether based on the Tradition of the Elders. The great merit of Marcion as a religious teacher is that he felt the charm of the Gospel message apart from the sanction of the Old Testament. Ephraim starts off his polemic against Marcion by appealing to the miracles of the Exodus, and to alleged confirmations of Old Testament wonders in the archives of Egypt and Babylon, an argument which now only raises a smile. But Marcion's position is not similarly affected by modern discovery: the God to Whom he gave his allegiance was always outside of this visible world, and if the visible world has been found not to be geocentric that matters less to him than to those whose God had His throne "above the bright blue sky."

Mani followed Marcion in two points: his treatment of the Old Testament and the organization of his disciples.

Marcion rejected the Old Testament in the sense of regarding it as inspired Scripture. The God of the Old Testament, the God of the Jews, was not his God. But the narratives of Genesis as retold by him played a great part in his religious theory. Similarly Mani, as we have seen, has a great deal to tell in the Epistle to Patticius about Adam and Eve. The story is entirely altered and a host of fantastic features accompany it, but apart from the tale in Genesis it never would have been told at all. Even the order of creation—plants, animals, men—follows the Bible story. As Mani took Bardaisan's cosmology and mythologized it, so he seems to have taken Marcion's theory of the origin of man and mythologized that.

Still clearer is his debt to Marcion seen in organization. To Marcion, as to Mani, all generation was abhorrent. It was a doing of the works of the Creator, a Potentate from whose allegiance he, Marcion, had escaped. Marriage to the Marcionite was marriage to Christ, and the married man or woman who desired to be baptized into the Marcionite Church had to renounce the earthly partner. But this rule in practice was not quite so severe as it sounds to our ears. The Marcionite catechumen, the unbaptized adherent of Marcion's religion, was given a higher status than the mere adherent in the Catholic Church. He was permitted to attend the Eucharist without communicating, and most Marcionites seem to have delayed their baptism, regarding it rather as a preparation for the life to come than as a means of grace for living a Christian life in this world. But this is exactly the organization of the Manichees into the Elect and the Hearers, the Elect who had abandoned marriage and property, and the Hearers one of whose chief religious duties was to provide food for the Elect, food which as Faustus the Manichee tells us they regarded as truly sacramental[1].

In regarding as Marcionite this organization into full members who eschew marriage and

---

[1] See above, p. 42.

recognized adherents who may marry, we are following the lead of S. Ephraim, but it must not be forgotten that Ephraim's own orthodox Church had at least tended to be organized on very similar lines. "He whose heart is set to the state of matrimony, let him marry before baptism, lest he fall in the spiritual contest and be killed," says Aphraates[1], writing in the Tigris valley as late as 345. In Syriac 'holy' and 'continent' are synonyms; so far as I can see, it was not till a couple of generations after the conversion of Constantine that the social organization of the Church in Mesopotamia was very different from that of the Marcionites. The rank and file of the baptized laity were called the Sons of the Covenant, living in the world in their own homes but not of it, very much like the Manichaean Elect.

The theory of Ephraim that Mani's system is properly to be regarded as derived from those of Marcion and Bardaisan is strongly supported by what we read in the *Fihrist*, although it is evident that the author of that invaluable work was not very well informed as to the real opinions of either of these Christian thinkers. In giving Mani's date he gives the date of Marcion and Bardaisan, evidently because these three names were grouped together in his authority[2]. Still more important is the fact that the first chapter of Mani's work *The Book of the Mysteries* (of which a Table

[1] See *Early Eastern Christianity*, p. 126 ff.
[2] So also Mas'ūdī, in the passage quoted by Flügel, p. 356.

of Contents is given in the *Fihrist*) was entitled 'Concerning the Bardesanians.' We see from this, that in explaining his own Religion Mani felt at once the impulse to start from what Bardaisan and the followers of Bardaisan had taught.

Let us now turn and see how much of all this theory of Manichaean origins is borne out by the newly-found documents of the Manichees themselves. One preliminary observation may be made. Our documents come from Turkestan, they were written for the use of people whose language and culture was Turkish. The documents that are not written in Turki are in a dialect of Middle-Persian, *i.e.* a dialect of the national language of the Sasanian Empire. At a somewhat later period than most of the Manichaean scraps we find Christian fragments which must have belonged to a Nestorian mission, but it is practically certain that the Nestorians exercised no influence on Manichaean literature. The extraneous influences to which this Turkestan Manichaean literature were exposed were Buddhistic from Thibet in the south, Chinese from the east, and Persian from the west. All the Syriac elements, and *a fortiori* the Greek elements, must have been there from the beginning, from the time of Mani and his immediate successors. If in dealing with Manichaean sources from Roman Africa we have to be on our guard lest Christian and Biblical elements should be only a local importation, brought in because the African Manichees were living in a Christian land, in Turkestan it is Persian and Buddhistic elements that are likely to be local and recent: the Christian elements will be original constituents of Mani's religion.

In these fragments from Turkestan the name of Bardaisan does not occur. Directly polemical literature indeed is only represented in the isolated scraps by a single ill-preserved pair of leaves, called M 28 by Professor F. W. K. Müller, and edited by him on pp. 94–5 of his *Handschriften-Reste aus Turfan*, II (1904). Hardly more than twenty short lines are legible, or at least have been transcribed, but in the course of these the writer attacks those who worship Fire and say that Ormuzd and Ahriman are Brothers; next he turns to the Christians who call Mary's Son (*Bar Maryam*) the Son of Adōnay, and says that they too, like the Fire-worshippers, will go into the Hell they have made for themselves; and then the fragment breaks off in the middle of the next sentence, which is directed against 'the God of Marcion.' It is a pity that more of the piece is not legible, but what survives is enough to shew that Marcion's system was important to this Manichaean theologian, if only by way of conscious opposition.

There are several direct references to Gospel events and to the teaching of Jesus in our Manichaean fragments, some agreeing with and others somewhat differing from the text of our Gospels. It may be said at once, to avoid any misconception, that there is no reason to suppose that the

Manichees preserved any independent tradition of the Gospel History. But it is a matter of importance to our view of Manichaeism to know from what sort of sources their knowledge of such things was derived. Prof. Müller points out that several of the peculiarities of the fragment M 18 (Müller, II, pp. 34 f., 109) seem to come from the apocryphal 'Gospel of Peter,' and as the proper names in M 18 have characteristically Syriac forms we seem here to go back to a lost Syriac translation of the Gospel of Peter. The fragment, which consists of the upper half of a leaf, has the headlines 'Hymns' and 'On the Crucifixion.' It runs thus:

.... "Truly He is the Son of God!" And Pilate answered: "I indeed am unconcerned in the blood of this Son of God." The centurions and soldiers (*Qatriyōnān va 'istratiyōtan*) then received command from Pilate: "Keep this secret," and the Jews gave a (?) promise. But he shews that on the first day of the week at cockcrow came Maryam, Shalōm, Maryam and many other women; they brought sweet herbs and nard. Near to the grave were they coming they....angel......as did Maryam, Shalōm and 'Arsanī'āh (*sic*). When the two angels said to them: "Seek not the Living among the dead! Jesu's word remember; how in Galilee He taught you 'They will give me up and have me crucified; on the third day from the dead I shall rise.' On this (?) afternoon go to Galilee, and bear the news to Simon and the others...."

The first part of this curious passage agrees, as Müller points out (p. 109), with the Gospel of Peter: the latter part does not do so, agreeing more with Luke xxiv, with touches from Mark (*e.g.* the name of 'Shalom'), yet not exactly with what we know of the Diatessaron. Probably the work, the headlines notwithstanding, was a controversial writing, and these are extracts from Christian writings, perhaps designed to shew inconsistencies in the orthodox account of the Passion.

Much the same may be said of M 132, which contains references to John xviii 36 ("My kingdom is not of this world") and to Matt. xxvii 29 f. (the Crown of Thorns, etc.), though perhaps here the intention is more in evidence, *viz.* to shew that Jesus laid no claim to rule[1] "in the House of Jacob and in the race of Israel[2]."

The use of the Gospel in the great apocalyptic fragment labelled M 475–477–482–472; 470; 473 is different. Here we are dealing with the *teaching* of Jesus, and we can gather how it was accepted by the Manichees with a characteristic perversion. The first four of these leaves follow in the above order, as is clear from the headlines (Müller, p. 10); 470 and 473 seem to have belonged to the same book, but there are no external indications where they came in it. M 482 *r.* and 472 *r.* are inscribed *Shābuḥragān,* so that we have either a fragment of Mani's famous work, or a quotation from it. M 477 *v.* is inscribed *Dō Būn Vazurg, i.e.* "The Two Great Roots" (or "Principles"), and M 470 *r.* has "...Ādūr Vazurg," i.e. "...the Great Fire." The actual contents agree with the headlines, in

---

[1] The word is broken away (Müller, ii 36).
[2] The fragment has *Sara'el*: see below.

fact a passage in the *Fihrist* (Flügel, p. 101) seems to be based on the text preserved in M 470[1]. In the middle of M 482 *r*. is a break of four blank lines, marking a new section: the text is badly preserved and no continuous translation can be made, but the subject is the End of the World according to the teaching of Mani. We read in M 482 about the New Aeon or Kingdom and the 'housing' (*bunīstān*) of the Demons; evidently this refers to the Prison or Grave that Ban, the Heavenly Builder, is to build in order to confine the Powers of Darkness in their own region[2]. We go on and find a reference to the Moon-God, in M 472 references to the 'Ship' (of Light) and to the Sun-God, and in M 470, as I said just now, we have a direct parallel to the *Fihrist*. All this belongs to the regular Manichaean circle of ideas. But it is preceded by a full paraphrase of Matt. xxv 31–46, the Christian picture of the Last Judgement with the righteous on the right and the wicked on the left, and the Headlines read "Concerning the Judgement" | "Of the Son of Man."

The tale is told almost in the words of the Gospel. Characteristically the 'sheep' and 'goats' are not named, for Manichees have nothing to do with the lower animals, but the Divine Lord of the world says to the 'righteous' on his right hand "I was hungry, thirsty, naked, sick, bound, in

---

[1] This is the fragment that also mentions the 1468 years of the World-Conflagration.

[2] See especially Mitchell, I, pp. xxx, xlvii, lxxv.

prison, a stranger, and ye gave me help," just as in the Gospel, and the righteous answer in surprise "When, Lord, did we do this?" together with the corresponding words to the wicked. It is, in fact, a paraphrastic quotation from the Christian Gospel, and when it comes to the end in the middle of M 482 *r*. (p. 16) there is the Rubric "Here endeth the Coming of the Life-Giver[1]," a title of our Lord very common in Syriac Christian literature.

I venture to suggest that the Manichee interpretation of the passage was the quite definite one that the deciding factor in the Last Day will be whether or no men and women have fed and clothed and succoured the Manichee Elect. In a Turkish fragment published by v. Le Coq (*Manichaica* III, p. 11) we read that "Mashiḥa the Burkhān," *i.e.* Jesus the Divine Prophet, has deigned to say that whoever [does not grudge] his property and possessions, but gives it as alms to the needy Elect (*dintar*), even if thereby he goes hungry, he will receive it as his eternal treasure. (p. 12) "Yea, with a single heart believe that one piece of thy bread, one cup of thy water, will not lose its reward!" Here quite clearly what is left undetermined in the Gospel is made quite definite: the 'brethren' of the heavenly Messiah are the Elect Manichees.

The exclusiveness of Manichaeism is one of its

[1] *Ḥanẓapt 'amadīshnīy 'ī Zīndkar*, which would be in Syriac ܐܬܐ ܕܡܚܝܢܐ ܕܢܚܣܠ.

weakest sides. It is decidedly more exclusive than Catholic Christianity, and in this respect it is more like the Novatians of old and the tendency represented by the Plymouth Brethren of recent times. In justice to the Manichees it must be remembered that they were almost always a persecuted minority. But the fact still remains, that their theory of Religion was exclusive, whatever their practice may have been.

From Polemics let us turn to Worship. It is evident that there was a good deal of 'worshipping of Angels' among the Manichees, but how much real worship, how much *hyperdulia*, how much magic and superstition is implied it would be difficult to say. Raphael (spelt *Rūpa'ēl*), Gabriel, Michael and Sarael all appear: these obviously have been simply taken over from Christian sources and afford another proof of the large part that such sources played in Manichaean *origines*. The last name appears to be a miswriting of 'Israel,' to which corresponds Jacob the Angel (*Yāqōb prēstag*), who is called the 'chief of the angels[1].' With the rejection of the Old Testament was no doubt connected a gross ignorance of Jewish history. Other angels are Narsūs, Nastīqūs, Bar Sīmūs and Qaptīnūs: I fear I have failed to find out anything about these personages. It is noteworthy that no references are made

[1] A list is given Müller, II, p. 45: the Angel Jacob is invoked, p. 56.

in these fragments to the *Splenditenens* or the *Atlas*.

One of the most striking varieties of the Manichaean hymn-forms is the *Sanctus*, for which they used the Syriac word *Ḳādōsh*[1]. Thus in M 75 (Müller, p. 70) we have as part of a Hymn: "Holy, holy, holy! Holy, holy, holy, to Thy glorified Kingdom! Holy, holy, holy, to Thee, Father! Holy, to Thy exalted Name! Holy, holy, holy, to Thee, Father!" The Hymn goes on similarly to acclaim God's Thought and Word, from which all good thoughts and words come, and God's Spirit (or Wind) that blows in the Divine Kingdom. This use of *Ḳādōsh* ultimately comes no doubt from the Vision of Isaiah, but there is no evidence for any independent use of the Old Testament by Manichees. This Manichee Hymn is therefore an adaptation of Christian usage, and as such may be held to be the earliest surviving evidence for the liturgical use of the *Sanctus*, for the exclamation '*Ḳādōsh*' is not likely to have been taken from a Christian hymn *after* the Manichees were organized as a separate religion.

Similarly *Amen* is used as a cry of adoration: "Amen, to thee, first-born Apostle, Divine Lord Mānī, our Saviour!" (Müller, p. 70 n.).

Very frequently 'Jesus' (*Yīshō'* or *Yīshō*) and Mani are invoked together, *e.g.* "O Jesu! among the Gods first New Moon!....Shining God!

[1] Also spelt *kādōsh*, with the wrong *k*. I suppose it to represent ܩܰܕܺܝܫ (*abs.*), not the Hebrew קָדוֹשׁ.

...Thou art God and Full Moon, Jesus Lord, Full Moon of waxing glory!...Mani, new Full Moon!....Holy (*Ḳādōsh*), Jesu, cleanse my stains! Divine Lord Mani, deliver my soul! Holy, God, O Light, look upon me! Power, Wisdom, God, deliver Thou me![1]" Or again: "O Jesu, Virgin of Light! O Lord Mani! Do Thou make peace within me! O Light-bringer, deliver my soul out of this born-dead life, deliver my soul out of this born-dead life![2]" We may quarrel with the form of expression, both from the literary and the theological point of view, but it is impossible to spell through these ancient Middle-Persian ejaculations without being convinced that they once represented genuine religious emotion.

The main object of the last few paragraphs has been to shew how large an element in Manichaean phraseology is derived from Syriac, and consequently (if we place ourselves in Babylonia, where Mani lived) from the West. This is therefore a convenient place to note that in another Hymn (M 32, p. 62 f.) we find the 'Son of God' is invoked as "Oh, *Lamtēr!*" *i.e.* the Greek word λαμπτήρ, and "Oh, *Safsēr!*" *i.e.* σαμψήρα. It is very odd to find the latter word in this form on Persian ground, for it is ultimately derived from the Persian *Shamshēr*, a scimitar, which passed into Syriac in the form *saphsērā*, from

[1] M 176, pp. 60–62 (extracts).
[2] M 38, p. 77.

93

which the Manichaean hymn-writer must have taken it. Possibly indeed the Manichee use of the word as a religious term is derived from the Syriac text of Hebr. iv 12. Another Greek word, transliterated into Syriac and then taken over by Mani, is *Paraclete*. This does not happen to occur in the Turkestan fragments, but that Mani really did regard himself as the Paraclete (Syriac *Pāraklēṭā*) whose coming had been foretold by Jesus is attested not only in the *Fihrist* and the Acts of Archelaus, but also now by Ephraim (Mitchell, ii, p. xcviii).

As is only natural, the Syriac and Syriac-Greek influence is more apparent in the Persian than in the Turkish fragments, for the Turkish documents are translations or adaptations from the Persian, and foreign terms and phrases tend to be dropped at every fresh translation.

If we had Mani's Syriac writings in full, preserved in the Syriac dialect in which they were originally written, there can be little doubt, I am sure, that the Greek element would be seen to be larger than appears from our Persian and Turkish fragments, which are after all only a small portion of what was once an extensive literature. It is no wonder if in the bits of it that have so unexpectedly come to light particular terms like *Paraclete* do not happen to be preserved. Similarly there is no mention of the *Bolos* referred to at the end of Lecture II. Nor again do we find the curious Manichee term for the Sun and Moon as

Receivers of the Light, which is preserved by Ephraim, *viz.* '*Hypodectae*[1],' a Greek word not very common in literature, but no doubt only too familiar to the provincials, for it means 'receivers of taxes.'

A Greek word that does not appear in the Turkestan fragments, or elsewhere certainly in Manichaean literature, is *Hyle* ὕλη. Ephraim seems to declare that *Hyle*, a word unknown to the Church, is in all three of the heretical systems of Marcion, Bardaisan and Mani[2], but it is only in Marcion's system that the term plays any great part, and most likely Ephraim only means to assert that the idea of *Hyle*, *viz.* an eternal, uncreated, unspiritual Element, is present in all three systems. As Flügel points out (p. 192), Mani does not speak of 'Matter' but of 'the Dark,' as also did Bardaisan. It is likely, however, that Greek-speaking Manichees may have used ὕλη as an equivalent for what Mani meant by 'the Dark.' It is inaccurate, of course; much nearer to the thought than *Hyle* is Alexander of Lycopolis's ἄτακτοσ κίνησισ, or as we might say in more modern terminology "atoms, vortices, electrons, not subject to natural laws," and consequently centres of real anarchy.

One isolated sign of Western influence deserves separate mention. Among the first of the Turfan

---

[1] ܩܘܕܟܝܐ ὑποδέκται, Mitchell, I, pp. xxxvi, xlii; see II, p. cxl.

[2] Mitchell, I, p. xcix.

fragments published was a single leaf, numbered M 97, which Prof. Müller recognized as a passage from the 'Shepherd of Hermas[1].' The four narrow columns correspond to *Similitude* IX, 4, 6 f., 18–25, and refer to the building of the Tower and the explanation of the Twelve Hills. The Persian text does not differ in essentials from the Greek, but it is much more compressed, in fact it must have been not a full translation but an epitome of the prolix original: the leaf which survives covers a section towards the end of the work, so that we may infer that the whole of the *Shepherd* was represented in the Manichee text. The specially odd part about the matter is that, so far as we know, the 'Shepherd of Hermas' was not current in Syriac. I venture to suggest that an explanation of the appearance of this rendering or epitome among the Persian-speaking Manichees is a result of their missions in the West, and that it points to a curious confusion between Hermas, the humble but inspired Christian slave, and Hermes Trismegistus. We know from Ephraim (Mitchell, II, p. xcviii) that the Manichees adduced Hermes along with Plato and Jesus as 'Heralds of the Good One to the world,' and Hermes Trismegistus is named with honour by the Manichee Faustus in Africa (Aug. *c. Faust.* XIII 1). When therefore some Western Manichee came across a book of revelations by 'Hermas' he may very well have

[1] F. W. K. Müller, in *Sitzungsberichte* of the Berlin Academy for 1905, pp. 1077–83.

thought it was the Seer and Prophet whom he had long been taught to revere. In any case the surviving fragment is one more proof of the influence of the West upon Manichaeism in general.

Before leaving this part of the subject I want once more to define the point I desire to make. No one can study the Manichaean fragments from Turkestan without being conscious of the influence of Buddhism in many of the documents, and there can be little doubt that Buddhist ideas, mythology and literature had a great share in the general civilization of the Manichaean communities in that part of the world. In the *Sitzungsberichte* of the Berlin Academy for 1909 v. Le Coq published a Turkish fragment (T II, D 173 *e*), which goes far to shew that the famous story of Barlaam and Joasaph, so popular all over the Christian world in mediaeval times, reached the West through a Manichee channel, or rather that it was through the Manichees that it reached the Arabic-speaking world and so became known to Greeks in Western Syria[1]. In speaking of this important fragment v. Le Coq says (p. 1204): "I would regard this leaf as a proof that an important place is occupied by Buddhism in the syncretistic religious system of Mani (at any rate in these regions)." The last six words, though v. Le Coq puts them in a

---

[1] The affiliation may shortly be expressed by saying that *Bodhisattva* became *Bodisav* among the Manichees, but it is by a confusion in Arabic script that *Bodisav* became *Yoasaf*.

bracket, make all the difference. Buddhism had been long at home in Turkestan before the Manichees established themselves there (v. Le Coq, p. 1213), and though the new Religion must have won many converts it was influenced by the religion it for a time displaced, just as it was influenced by Catholic Christianity in North Africa and the West generally. But I have been specially concerned in these Lectures with the original teaching of Mani, with the missionary Religion that fought for a century-and-a-half on almost equal terms, as it seemed, with the Church of the Roman Empire. In this Religion I see no sure trace of Buddhism as a formative element. Buddha is mentioned by Mani with respect, as he mentions Plato and Hermes Trismegistus. He knew very little, I believe, about these thinkers except their great names.

The Buddhistic influence in the documents from Turkestan should not surprise us. It was a half-Buddhist country, and the wholly Buddhist countries were near at hand. The Syriac, and still more the Greek elements, on the other hand, must have been brought by the Manichees themselves; in other words, they are an integral part of the Manichaeism of Babylonia, the Manichaeism of Mani himself. In the circumstances of their transmission I think we have some reason to be surprised that these Syriac and Greek elements are so large: they seem to me to shew that S. Ephraim was right in looking to the non-Catholic elements

in Syriac-speaking Christianity, in other words to
Bardaisan and Marcion, as the active sources of
Mani's inspiration.

And now that we have come to the end of our
survey, what are we to say of the Religion of the
Manichees as a whole? Why had it so successful
a career? Has it anything to say to us now? When
Mani came forward as the Prophet of his new
Religion we must surely recognize that there was
much in it to appeal to human religious instincts.
It is natural to wish to be a son of the Light.
Children cry in the Dark, and 'a pleasant thing
it is to behold the sun,' even in sultry Mesopotamia. Moreover Mani seemed to his followers
to have explained what the old religions which
had gone before him had only hinted at. But
beyond these generalities the philosophy which
underlies the whole structure seems to me to have
even now a certain attraction, still perceptible
through its fantastic barbarian trappings. The
Religion of Mani is an attempt to explain the
presence of Evil in the world we live in, and it
does combine practical pessimism with ultimate
optimism—perhaps the most favourable atmosphere for the religious sentiment. It is true that
the Manichees thought of the world we live in as
the result of a regrettable accident, so that no true
improvement is possible till it is altogether
abolished. As regards this world they are frankly
pessimistic: it was bad to begin with, and it will

go from bad to worse. But they believed that Light is really greater and stronger than the Dark, that in the end all that was good in their being would be collected in the domain of Light, a realm altogether swayed by Intelligence, Reason, Mind, good Imagination, and good Intention; and though at the same time there would always exist another region, dark, and dominated by unregulated Desire, it would only be peopled by beings for whom such a region was appropriate, and they would be separated off for ever from invading the region of Light and so producing another Smudge, such as our present world essentially is, according to the Manichaean view.

The world—a Smudge; that is the view of Mani, and it was one which he shared with Bardaisan. He shared with him the concepts of the attack by the primordial Dark upon the Pure Elements; the consequent Mixture, or (as I have ventured to call it) the Smudge; the control of the damage by the Good God, and a plan for the eventual redemption of souls from the power of the Dark element. The idea is that this is the best of all possible worlds,—considering the circumstances, considering the ruin out of which it had to be constructed. I have placed at the head of this Lecture a quotation from a thoughtful work by a well-known modern clergyman, occupied not with the study of dead Religions but with the life of men and women in present-day industrial conditions. The conclusion to which Canon Green has come is so near the fundamental assumption of the Religion of the Manichees that we may well ask whether Mani and Bardaisan may not have some right in their contention. Who knows?

I would conclude, not with a query to which none of us can have an answer, but rather with a suggestion as to the influence of Manichaeism upon our traditional ideas about the origin of Evil. "Of *Man's* first disobedience and the fruit Of that forbidden tree" we learn from S. Paul; the sin of Adam and its effects was a doctrine common to all Christendom. But Adam was not the only great offender. What are we to say of Satan and his companions? When and why did the Angels fall?

In the answers to this question given by ancient Christian thinkers we can distinguish three stages. First, there is the answer given in pre-Christian days by the Book of Enoch, which tells us that the Fall of the Angels took place after Man had multiplied upon the earth, and the Sons of God saw the daughters of men that they were fair, and they took them wives of all that they chose. Thus the Angels fell through *Lust*, many years after Adam's disobedience: this is the answer given by Justin Martyr, by Athenagoras, by Clement of Alexandria and by Tertullian[1]. A

---

[1] See Gen. vi 1 ff., Enoch vi ff.: also Just. *Ap.* II 5; Athenag. 24; Clem. Al. *Paed.* II 2 and *Stromat.* III 329, v 401; Tert. *de Cult. Fem.* I 2.

second answer tells us that Satan fell through *Envy*, envy of Man, God's new formation, and so Satan tempted Adam to do wrong. According to this, therefore, the first beginning of evil was after the creation of Man, but before he transgressed: this answer is found in Irenaeus and Cyprian[1]. The third answer tells us that Satan fell through *Pride*, and this is the answer generally given. It does not appear, however, before Eusebius, but from Eusebius onward it is generally alleged, *e.g.* by Athanasius, by Cyril of Jerusalem, by Gregory Nazianzen and by Chrysostom[2].

But the writer through whom this opinion most won acceptance is Augustine. He does not know indeed how the evil Will came in (*de Ciuit. Dei*, XII 7)—how could he?—but it seems that he knows everything else. It is amusing or pathetic, according as we take it, to follow Augustine through the Eleventh Book of the 'City of God' and mark how he proves step by step that the Angels must have been created before the Stars (see Job xxxviii 7), not on the third or the second Day, but when God said "Let there be Light!" (*de Ciuit. Dei*, XI 9); and when He divided between the Light and the Darkness He distinguished between the Good and the Bad Angels (XI 18, 33),

---

[1] Iren. *Haer.* IV 40, 3 and *Epideixis*, 16; Cypr. *de Zelo et Liuore*, 4.

[2] Euseb. *Praep.* VII 16; Athan. *de Virgin.* 5; Cyr. Hier. *Cat.* II 3; Greg. Naz. *Arc.* 6.

for Satan fell at once, though the evil was not immediately apparent.

Thus according to this view, as Saint Columba says:

Superbiendo ruerat   Lucifer quem formauerat,

and evil came about by Pride before ever Man was created. According to Augustine, therefore, Man was formed in a Universe where there were already Two Powers, God and Satan, and in the first battle between these two principles of Light and Dark the first man came to grief. Is not this the Manichaean presentation? I venture to suggest that Augustine was still carrying about with him more Manichaean ideas than he was conscious of. Those who look for it can still trace the Manichaean imagery in this 11th book of Augustine's great work. Augustine knew that Darkness was no more than the absence of Light, but for all that when in XI 33 he is making a contrast between the two Angelical Societies, the one *tranquil* in its *luminous* piety, the other *turbulent* with its *dark* cupidities and *smoking* with the unclean mouth of its own loftiness, he uses language with a curiously Manichaean ring. And while he was doing this he was binding the imaginations of fifty generations to come. The learned construction of Augustine passed into the poetical conceptions of Avitus, of Columba, and finally (with a characteristic perversion) into those of Milton.

It is not only a question of primitive myth; it

is a theory of conduct, for this view of human life taught that Man went and still goes wrong because he had always lived in a Dualistic world, a world where the Light and the Dark existed in opposition before Man was, and where though the Light is stronger than the Dark it will never quite illuminate it altogether. I venture to suggest that a prime factor in the reasons that led to the spread of these ideas was the preaching that began on the 20th of March, 242, in Babylonia and that for a time made a convert of S. Augustine.

APPENDICES

I. THE MANICHAEAN HIERARCHY

THE names of the various grades among the Manichees are perhaps not very important, especially as we do not know the special functions of the higher grades. But as the details given by our authorities seem not to be quite harmonious I have brought them together in a separate Note. Prof. Müller in the Berlin *Abhandlungen* for 1912 (*Ein Doppelblatt*, p. 37) gives the five grades in a Table thus:

PERSIAN NAME	AUGUSTINE	FIHRIST (95)
ḥamōzāg	*magister*	Lehrer
ʿispasag	*episcopus*	Dienender
maḥistag	*presbyter*	Verwaltender
χrōḫχvān	*electus*	Wahrhaftiger
niyōšāg	*auditor*	Zuhörer

But when we come to examine the authorities we find that each list contains an element of conjecture. The Persian List comes from a Colophon, in which the writer invokes blessings on three Manichaean dignitaries : these are no doubt in order of dignity. He calls himself a χrōḫχvān, *i.e.* 'caller' or possibly 'preacher.' This may very well be the name of an office rather than of a grade in religion, for all the other evidence suggests that the Persian term for an Elect Manichee was *'ardāv*, *i.e.* 'true' or 'genuine,' corresponding to *ẕaddīḳ*. Of the other names, *niyōshāg* 'hearer' is added by Prof. Müller from elsewhere, as it does not happen to come in the

Colophon at this point; *'ispasag* may very well be a Persian adaptation of *episcopus*; *ḥamōẓāg*, so far as I know, does not occur again in the literature hitherto published, but several of the Turkish documents mention the *maḥistag* (or *mayistag*)[1].

Of the names mentioned in the *Fihrist* (text in Flügel, p. 64) the last causes no difficulty; the last but one is *ṣiddīḳ*, corresponding to the Syriac *ẓaddīḳ* and to 'faithful'; the third is *ḳasīs* (*ḳissīs*), the regular word for a Christian priest and therefore exactly equivalent to Augustine's *presbyter*. The second word in the *Fihrist* is *mushammis*, which seems to be a rendering of the Syriac *mshammshānā*, 'a deacon': it is possible that our Moslem writer has made a mistake in the nomenclature of an alien religion; if not, this term may have been used by the Manichaean 'bishops' in accordance with the principle enunciated in Matt. xx 26, like *seruus seruorum* in the Pope's style.

Finally, the concordance of the *Fihrist's* 'teacher' (*mu'allim*) with Augustine's *magister* makes it clear that the highest dignitary in the Manichee hierarchy was the Doctor, but whether the Manichees permanently restricted the number to twelve (Aug. *de Haeres.* 46, quoted in Flügel, p. 298) is not known.

It should be added that Ephraim four times uses the term *ḳphalpālā* (ܟܦܠܦܠܐ a trisyllable, vocalization uncertain) for the highest Manichee grade. The word occurs in Mitchell, II 205, 206,

[1] *E.g.* v. Le Coq, *Manichaica* III, pp. 9, 35 f.

I. THE MANICHAEAN HIERARCHY

as well as in certain Hymns (ES 3, 100 B, ESL 1, 105). According to the first of these passages there might be as few as Five of them in the world. The derivation of the term is quite obscure: possibly it is a fanciful formation from κεφαλή, as if one should say a 'chapterer' for one who is at the head.

II. THE FIVE PURE ELEMENTS

THE Primal Man, according to the Manichaean story, was arrayed with the Five Pure Elements as a sort of panoply when he went forth to fight with the Demon of the Dark. Ephraim speaks of them as ܙܝܘܢܐ, usually transliterated zīwānē and supposed to mean 'brilliant.' Four of them were Light, Wind, Water, Fire, but Ephraim curiously avoids naming the fifth (Mitchell, 1, p. lxxix : see also 11, p. cxxxiv). Indeed I do not know of any Syriac source that names the fifth Element at all. On the other hand it is given as *aer* by Augustine (*c. Faust.* 11 3), and in the *Acta Archelai* VII as ὕλη[1], which ever since Beausobre has been regarded as a mere palaeographical corruption of ἀήρ. The Arabic (Flügel, *Fihrist*, p. 87) gives النسيم 'the gentle breeze' or 'zephyr.'

The Manichaean documents from Turfan tell us that the name of this fifth Element was *pravahr* in Middle-Persian and *tintura* in Turkish. More-

---

[1] So Epiphanius : the Latin has *maria*, no doubt a corruption of *materia*.

over there survives one important text which
seems to shew that the pure elements were sometimes enumerated as Four, sometimes as Five, a
fact which may explain the curious absence of a
fifth term in our Syriac documents. In Müller,
Handschriften-Reste aus Turfan II, p. 38, we read
(M 98, l. 8 ff.) :

He [(?) the Heavenly Jesus, or the 'Living Spirit'[1]]
  out of the Wind and Light Water and Fire
    which had been refined from the Mixture
  two Light-carriers
     that of the Sun   out of the Fire and Light
       with 5 walls of aether wind light water and fire
       and 12 doors and houses 5 and thrones 3
       and soul-collecting angels 5
       in the fiery wall
  and that of the Moon-God out of the Wind and Water
      with 5 walls of aether wind light water and fire
      and 14 doors and houses 5 and thrones 3
      and soul-collecting angels 5
      in the watery wall
       made and arranged.

Prof. Müller translates *rôshan-rahê* by 'Fahrzeug,'
and supposes them to be Augustine's 'ships of
Light,' but the description of them suggests to
me rather the heavenly Orbits or Roads along
which Sun and Moon are made to travel. It is
to be noted that these 'Light-orbits' were called
in Syriac ᚷᚷᚷ, rendered by Cumont 'circles'
(see Cumont, *Recherches* I 31)[2]. Prof. Bang in his
edition of the *Khuastuanift*, p. 216, note 2, suggests

[1] See Cumont, I 31.
[2] Note that here in the text of Theodore bar Konai the
word 'Light' has fallen out after 'Wind.'

II. THE FIVE PURE ELEMENTS

'Feldlager' or 'Pfalz,' but the word means literally 'Light-way,' and after all the obvious fact about the Sun and Moon is that they go along definite paths in the sky which they never leave ; it was natural therefore to suppose that these paths must be bounded by heavenly walls.

But I am not here so directly concerned with the exact figure and plan of these grandiose constructions as with the fact that while the elements refined out of the 'mixture' are enumerated as 'Wind and Light, Water and Fire,' the 'walls' are made of the *Five* elements Aether, Wind, Light, Water and Fire. Was no 'Aether' refined out of the mixture? Was the Aether never retained by the Archons? In any case there seems to be a hesitancy or inconsistency of presentation, which goes some way to account for the silence of our Syriac texts about this 'Aether.'

It is worth notice that all the texts which enumerate Five Elements (*Fihrist*, this Persian text, *Khuastuanift* 34–37, and the Turkish texts edited by v. Le Coq, *Manichaica* III, p. 16) enumerate them in the same order, except the corrupt text of the *Acta Archelai*.

Flügel points out (pp. 187, 200) that Shahrastānī treats the 'Air' or 'Aether' as the 'spirit' moving in the 'bodies' of the other Light-elements. Shahrastānī's words are : "The species [of the Light] are five ; four of them are substances (ابدان 'bodies'), and the fifth their spirit (روحها). And the substances are Fire, Light, Wind and

Water, and their spirit is the Zephyr (النسيم), and this moves in these bodies" (Shahrastānī, ed. Cureton, p. 189). The word for 'wind' is ريح, different from that for 'spirit,' which is روح. In Syriac, of course, the same word ܪܘܚܐ is used for both.

It is in accordance with this view that the *Fihrist* says (Flügel, p. 94) that this Element (النسيم) is the Life of the world, and the same idea, no doubt, is reflected in the Persian and Turkish names. Both syllables of *tintura* seem to mean 'life' or 'living,' and *pravahr* seems to mean 'substance' or 'essence.' In other words these terms tell us as little of the physical meaning of this Element as 'eau-de-vie' does of brandy.

The Five pure Elements are called by Ephraim the Five *Zīwānē* (sing. *ẕīwānā*), and no doubt this is the proper Manichaean Syriac term. But what does it mean? We have only the consonantal text (ܙܝܘܢܐ), and as I said at the beginning of this Note it is generally supposed to mean 'the brilliant ones,' from *ẕīwā* 'splendour.' The *Khuastuanift*, which uses the curious expression 'Five-God' as the equivalent for *ẕīwānē*, says that of everything on earth the 'Five-God' is the Root, Foundation, Light, Strength, Body and Soul (ll. 45–48). This suggests to me that *ẕīwānā* must originally have meant something more significant than 'brilliant.' Is it not possible that it is really a Middle-Persian word meaning 'living one'?

II. THE FIVE PURE ELEMENTS

The Persian for that is *ẕīwandag* (Müller, II, pp. 35, 65) : it seems to me quite likely that the Syriac *ẕīwānā* is a Manichaean adaptation of this.

What makes this conjecture more probable is that the word *ẕīwānā* is used as a Manichee epithet for 'Jesus' in the text quoted by Theodore bar Konai. "Jesus the *ẕīwānā* came to Adam and waked him up from his death-slumber" (Cumont, I 46), going on to explain to him something of the doctrine about the *patibilem Iesum qui est uita ac salus hominum ab omni ligno suspensus (Ibid.* p. 48). It is obvious that in such a context 'brilliant' is out of place, while 'living' or 'life-giving' is exactly appropriate.

The complete answer to these questions cannot be made till we know what the correct Syriac equivalent was for the Element which was variously translated النسيم, *tintura* and *aer*.

III. MANICHEE FRAGMENTS IN SYRIAC

A FEW fragments in Manichaean script have turned up during the last few years in Egypt. They are all very small in extent, so small that no complete sentence survives, but they throw a curious side-light on the Manichaean literature and propaganda, and are of especial interest as preserving the only known specimens of the actual dialect of Aramaic used by Manichees, the language in which no doubt all the main works of Mani but one were composed.

The fragments fall into three groups : (*a*) the
British Museum Fragment; (*b*) Mr Crum's scraps;
(*c*) the Oxyrhynchus Fragments.

(*a*) Brit. Mus. Or. 6201 C (1).

This fragment consists of the inner part of two
conjugate vellum leaves. No whole line is completely preserved. A photograph was published
in the *J.R.A.S.* for April 1919 by W. E. Crum,
and a few words transcribed by him were recognized as Syriac by E. W. Brooks. The fragment
is thought to have come from Ashmunain.

col. A (=1 r)	col. D (=1 v)

No continuous translation can be made of this,
particularly as we do not know the length of the
complete lines of writing, but D 8 ("beloved
brothers") suggests a Homily. Note the stop at

the *beginning* of A 3 : this seems to be a Manichaean habit, found in MSS. from Turfan. Possibly the subject may have been an exposition of sayings of Mani, so that A 9, 10 may have run "That *Mani* said thus : 'Do...'"

col. C (= 2 r)   col. B (= 2 v)

Here again no translation is possible, but the language is clearly Syriac. Specially noteworthy is *bar shā'theh*, *i.e.* 'immediately' (B 7), a regular Edessene Syriac idiom, not I believe found in Jewish Aramaic. Note also the imperf. formed with *n*, not *y*, just as in Edessene (B 8).

(*b*) Five tiny vellum scraps belonging to Mr W. E. Crum.

These are hitherto unpublished, and have kindly been lent to me for examination. They come from

Middle Egypt, and appear to have been used to bind some ancient Coptic MSS.

A. col. r 1 col. r 2

col. v 1 col. v 2

Blank

The most interesting word here is in v 1, line 1, for *āthalyā* means 'eclipse' (or possibly 'dragon,' as an astronomical term). The nature of the argument in the text cannot be recovered, but its subject was evidently astronomical.

B. This is a tiny vellum strip containing portions of eleven lines of writing, but only three or four letters are preserved in each line.

C. This an even smaller strip, containing portions of seven lines of writing. One of these lines contains the word ⟨⟩, *i.e.* 'Archon,' the well-known Manichaean term for the Demon of the Dark.

D and E are too small and broken to be read at all.

(*c*) The Oxyrhynchus Fragments.
These were edited by Professor Margoliouth

III. MANICHEE FRAGMENTS IN SYRIAC

in the *Journal of Egyptian Archaeology* for Oct. 1915, pp. 214-16. Unfortunately Prof. Margoliouth had misapprehended at least one sign in the Manichaean alphabet (ܣ), and the transcripts do not in all cases seem to have been revised by the facsimile, so that the tentative translations are for the most part rather misleading.

The fragments are now in the Bodleian Library (Syr. d 13 P, 14 P) and consist of ten small strips of papyrus, much torn and in places so much rubbed as to be illegible. I follow Prof. Margoliouth's numeration.

Bodl. Syr. d 14 (P).
1. Strip of one line.

ܟܬܘܒ ܩܘܒܠܬܟܘܢ ܟܬܘܒ ܕܝܢ ܟܬܐ [

..who knew not sin on your account sin

This is correctly recognized by Margoliouth as a quotation from 2 Cor. v 21, but he prefixes ܝܫܘܥ which is not in the ms., for the lost word in front of ܟܬܐ ends with ܥ, so that the missing word might be 'Jesus.' Margoliouth points out that the fragment agrees with the Peshitta text in substituting ὑμῶν for ἡμῶν, but differs from it in omitting ܗܘܐ after ܝܕܥ.

Here therefore, in this isolated scrap of Manichaean writing, is an agreement with the Syriac N.T. against all other critical authorities, one more instance of the dependence of the Manichees upon Syriac Christendom.

Margoliouth's ܠܒܪ belongs to the next column (on the *left*), now quite torn away.

2. Strip of three lines: in two columns, not as Margoliouth prints it in one.

[※ ܐܝܟ ܓܒܪ ܐܠܝܨ ܚܠܝܨ ܘܪ[ܕ]ܝܦ
[※ ܠܩܕܡ ܓܒܪ ܛܒ ܩܫܝܛ ܘ[
[ܛܐ ܐܢܐ ܒܪ ※ ܠܡܢܘ ܓܝܪ ܐܚܪܢ ܐܝܬ ܠܝ ܠܡܐܡܪ[ܘ

The signs between the columns may mark a quotation.

Translate:

like a man afflicted oppressed and persecuted..
before a man good true and....
For to whom else have I to say...

In line 2 Margoliouth read ܒܩܕܡ and ܘܫܝܛ, and the first word of line 3 ܠܡܢܗ.

This short text is grammatically interesting. The 'defective' spellings ܠܩܕܡ and ܐܚܪܢ are found elsewhere, *e.g.* in the Sinai Palimpsest, but the use of the 'absolute' in ll. 1 and 2 is against the peculiarly Edessene usage. Still more interesting is ܩܫܝܛ, which is the correct form, used also in Jewish and Palestinian Aramaic, in Arabic and in Hebrew, but in Edessene Syriac the root is spelt with ܬ (ܩܘܫܬܐ, etc.).

3. Strip with fragments of nine lines.

[ܟܠ]
ܐܬܐܠܝ ܟܠ ܕܗܘܐ ܒ[
ܐܚܕ ܘܡܕܒܪܐ ܠܡܫܝܚܐ[

]ܐܠܐ ܐܠܐ ܡܢ ܐܡܪ̈ܐܝܢ[

5]ܐܝܟ ܕܐܡܪ̈ܝܬ[

]ܒ

ܘܠ[*]ܪܝܪ̈ܐ ܐܠܐ. ܐܬܠܗ ܝܗܒܬܡ ؟ ؟

ܡ[*]ܝܘܪ̈ܘܬ ܒ * *

ܐܠ

Translate (ll. 2 and 3):

..There was afflicted every righteous man in [the world from] Adam even unto the Saviour [   ] But I say.....as I [have] said.....

The rest is unintelligible. In l. 7 ܐܬܠܗ *I will give him* is clear : possibly the line may mean *and to the [vul]ture I will give him.*

ܡܚܝܢܐ *Saviour* or *Life-giver* is a regular Syriac title for our Lord, and we have seen (p. 90) that it was used also by the Manichees.

Bodl. Syr. d 13 (P).

1. "Strip containing a few letters, wherein the word ܐܝ̈ܕܐ *hands* can be distinguished. Also some Coptic letters." So Margoliouth, but all the writing is clearly Greek. The letters read ܐܝ̈ܕܐ are the Greek letters ΚΔΙΟΝ. Above this is ΤΗΝ. At right angles to this the letters 1. ΠΕΤΔ and 2. ΤΕϹΤ are legible.

2, 3, 4. Very small fragments.

APPENDICES

5. Strip containing fragments of two columns.

ܬ ܟ. ܡܚܡ	ܟܢܝܟܐ * *	1
ܕ ܟܝܚܠ ܝܡ ܒܝܚܠ ܕ	* ܡ ܘܢܥܢܡ	2
ܟܝܨܚܠܕܚܠ	[ornament]	3
[illegible]	* * *	4
,,	* ܗ ܗ ܝܠܐ	5
,,	[cut away]	6–8
ܡܕܗ ܥܩܘܝ *	[,,]	9
[illegible or blank]	* ܟ ܟܘܐ ܕܚܒܚ ܚܡܚܣܪ	10
,,	ܟܕܗ ܟܢ ܟܠܢܠܘܕ ܟܚܡܟܕ ܚܡܨܝܐ	11
,,	ܟܐ[ܟ .ܡܚܒܚܡܝ ܚܠ ܟܝܟ	12

This is not continuous enough to translate. I print this, almost exactly agreeing with Margoliouth, because it is evidently written in regular Edessene or 'classical' Syriac, not Mandaean or some unknown Aramaic dialect.

6. Fragment.

* * ܘܟܝܡܚܒ*ܝ *
* ܟܝܡܘܚܡܚܚ ܚܒܡ ܟܡܚ
* ܝܟܐܠ ܠܝ ܣܠܝ ܛܘܩ

This of course is a mere incoherent fragment. I print it, because l. 2 is quite clear. The letters are as printed, viz. ḲBWZḲYA BSA, which cannot be translated, as Margoliouth does, 'a despised Cappadocian.'

118

III. MANICHEE FRAGMENTS IN SYRIAC
7. Fragment.

* * ܟܒܪܐ * *

ܐܪܥܐ * *

ܒܫܘܩ̈ܐ ܗܘ ܗܕܟܡܐ܂ ܠܚܣܝ܂ ܘ

Does the last line mean '*that shoe in the markets of Persia*'?

It is evident that mere scraps like the last two may easily offer insoluble riddles. But what is clear from the longer and more coherent fragments is that the language used is almost identical with classical Syriac, and that several known Manichaean peculiarities reappear in these tiny remains of the Manichee propaganda in Egypt.

IV. THE SOGHDIAN LECTIONARY

AMONG the remains of Buddhistic, Manichaean and Christian fragments discovered near Turfan in Chinese Turkestan are some leaves and parts of leaves of a Gospel Lectionary written in Syriac letters in the Soghdian language, a dialect of Middle-Persian. The leaves have been excellently transcribed and edited by Prof. F. W. K. Müller in the *Abhandlungen* of the Berlin Academy for 1912 (*Abh.* II, pp. 1–111)[1], who recognizes that they are fragments of a Lectionary, and that the Soghdian text is a translation from the Peshitta.

[1] F. W. K. Müller, *Soghdische Texte* I.

On going through the fragments I perceived that the Lectionary is the Nestorian one.

As the fragments are old (at least 10th cent.) and their origin so peculiar I have thought it worth while to collect the Lessons in their liturgical order, so as to shew what part of the Nestorian Lectionary is supported by this witness from the far North-East. As a basis of comparison I have taken the numbered sections in Camb. Univ. Libr. *Add.* 1975, a Gospel Lectionary written in A.D. 1586 for the Church of Mosul (Catal. of *C.U.L.*, pp. 58–80).

Of the 55 fragments edited by Prof. Müller, 49 belong to the Lectionary. They are contained on 23 leaves of which a certain number are conjugates. As the numbers given to the single fragments are haphazard I shall quote them also by Müller's pages (*e.g.* 67 r[1] = M 3).

The few instances in which the Fragments preserve the beginning of a Lesson with its Rubrics are alone enough to shew that they come from a Nestorian Lectionary, *e.g.* those for the 6th Sunday in Lent, or for Friday 'of the Confessors' (*i.e.* Friday after Easter). Where the Section (*shāḥā*) is given, the number always agrees with Gwilliam's numeration as collected from Peshitta MSS.

Frg. 64 v = Müller, p. 28 f., is the beginning of the whole book. No doubt the recto is blank, as is usual in Syriac MSS., and very likely it was preceded by one (or two) blank leaves as a guard.

---

[1] The full numeration is T. II, B. 67 r (or v): I give only the numbers, for short.

Lections of C.U.L. Add. 1975	Soghdian fragment	Extant verses	Kalendar dates	§§	§ 1
1	64 v = M 28-30[1]	Lk. i 1-4....	[1st] Sund. in Dec.		§ 1
		two leaves missing here			
3	38 rv = M 30-32	Lk. i 63-80	[3rd Sund. in Dec.]		
4	38 v = M 32	Matt. i 1- (*sic*)	4th Sund. in Dec.		§ 1
		....			
19	17 (ii) rv = M 57-60	Joh. i..19-28	[2nd Sund. after Epiph.]		
21	17 (ii) v = M 60-61	Joh. i 29-35....	[3rd] Sund. [after Epiph.] in § 1		
		......			
38	67 rv = M 3-4	Matt. v..30-33....	[M. 1st wk. in Lent]		
39	67 v = M 5	Matt. v 38-40....	T. [1st wk. in Lent]		
		......			
47	66 (ii) rv = M 17-21	Matt. xxi..28-43....	[4th Sund. in Lent]		
49	99 rv = M 61-64	Joh. v..25-40....	[T. mid-wk. in Lent][2]		
not read	12 (ii) rv = M 41-45	Lk. xvi..2-16	?		

1 64 r appears to be blank: this was the first written leaf of the Codex.
2 That this Lection must be placed here is confirmed by the signature ꝯ, *i.e.* the fragment was the first leaf of Quire 4.

Lections of *C.U.L.* Add. 1975	Soghdian fragment	Extant verses	Kalendar dates	§§
55	12 (ii) v = M 45	Joh. ix 39–	6th Sund. in Lent	in § 10
		......		
		one leaf missing here		
69	16 rv = M 50–52	Lk. xxiv 19–32	[T. after Easter]	
69	66 (iii) r = M 52–53	Lk. xxiv..32–34....	[T. after Easter]	
70	66 (iii) v = M 70–71	Joh. xv..18–20...	[W. after Easter]	
		two leaves missing here		
71	71 (i) r = M 5	Matt. x..14–15	[Th. after Easter]	in § 7
72	71 (i) rv = M 5–8	Matt. x 16–26	F. of the Confessors	
72	71 (ii) r = M 8–10	Matt. x 27–33....	F. of the Confessors	
73	71 (ii) v = M 78	Joh. xx..19–25....	[New Sunday][1]	
		two leaves missing here		
77	12 (iii) rv = M 71–75	Joh. xvi..20–32....	[4th Sund. of Easter]	
77	99ª r = M 76	Joh. xvi 33		
79	99ª r = M 76	Joh. xxi 1–...	[5th] Sund. of Easter	
79	99ª v = M 79	Joh. xxi..5–7....	[5th] Sund. of Easter	
		two leaves missing here		
80	66 (iv) r = M 77	Joh. xvii..24–26	[6th Sund. of Easter]	

[1] 71 (i) and 71 (ii) are conjugate leaves, still joined, and must have been the inside of a quire. The same is true of 34 (i) and 34 (ii).

81	66 (iv) rv = M 53–57	Lk. xxiv 36–47...	[Ascension Day]
87	12 (i) rv = M 34–38	Lk. x..34–42	[3rd Sund. of Apostles]
88	12 (i) v = M 32–33	Lk. vi 12–17...	4th Sund. [of App.] in § 6
97	34 (i) rv = M 65–70	Joh. ix..9–38...	[3rd Sund. of Summer]¹
	34 (ii) rv	,,	
104	66 (i) r = M 10–11	Matt. xiii..17–19...	[2nd Sund. of Elias]
105	66 (i) v = M 11–12	Matt. xiii 24–25...	[3rd Sund. of Elias]
	39 (i) rv = M 45–49	Lk. xix..15–27	
	39 (i) v = M 21–22	Matt. xxv 31–33	S. Barshabba in § 19
	39 (ii) rv = M 23–27	,, 33–45	²
	17 (i) r = M 12–13	,, 45–46	
	17 (i) rv = M 12–16	Matt. xvi 24–xvii 7...	[S. Sergiu]s and S. Bacchus
	X r = M 41	Lk. xiii..3–4...	
	X v = M 17	Matt. xx..17–19...	
	52 rv = M 38–40	Lk. xii..35–44	[See p. 124]
	52 v = M 40	Joh. v 19–	

¹ See footnote, p. 122.
² 39 (i) and 39 (ii) must have been the inside leaves of a quire.

Most of the Lessons agree exactly with the Nestorian use, where the beginnings or endings of the Lessons are preserved, but No. 4 begins at Matt. i 1, thus including the Genealogy, while the present Nestorian lesson begins at i 18. Immediately preceding No. 55 is Lk. xvi (1)–16, for which I do not know a Nestorian parallel, nor can I suggest an appropriate Lenten day. In 19 and 21, 77 and 79, Sunday lessons follow immediately on one another, omitting the week-day commemorations that come in between (in these cases those of the Evangelists and of the Maccabaean Martyrs). Evidently, therefore, the Commemorations were arranged at the end. Here, then, belongs the long continuous piece, containing the Lessons for the commemorations of S. Barsabbas (?) (ܒܪܫܒܐ) and of SS. Sergius and Bacchus. The former has the Commemoration for the Dead, and the latter that of the Syrian Doctors, which is also the old Lesson for SS. Peter and Paul, or very nearly. I do not know who is meant by Barsabbas; possibly the name is not read correctly. Before these two sets comes a Lesson ending with Lk. xix 27: this again seems a novelty.

The Lessons I have put at the end also belong to commemorations. At the end of Lk. xii 44 comes the catch-words in Syriac, as always in our MS., thus: "'A[men, amen, I say to you,] The Son [cannot] do aught,' as far as.... See at the Entry of the F[ast.] Commemoration of...."

IV. THE SOGHDIAN LECTIONARY

The text is Joh. v 19 : I take 'the Entry of the Fast' to be a scribe's error for Mid-Lent[1], and the reference to be to No. 49.

It is evident that these fragments keep very closely to the Nestorian Gospel Lectionary as known to us from MSS. of the 11th and succeeding centuries. We may conclude, therefore, that the Christians of Chinese Turkestan were closely allied in culture and organization to their brother Nestorians in Mesopotamia and the Tigris Valley. The literature they brought to that remote region is already known to us fairly well from other sources, and indeed it is not likely on general grounds that they would bring rare or antiquated books thither. When therefore we find at Turfan in Manichaean script extracts from the 'Shepherd of Hermas' or legendary amplifications of the Gospels, it is pretty certain that they belong to a Manichaean line of transmission, that they belong to what Mani and his earlier disciples took from Christian sources, not to what later Manichaeans may have from time to time assimilated from their Christian neighbours. In any case this Lectionary remains an interesting and authentic monument of Nestorian missionary activity, contemporary with the famous Chinese monument of Si-ngan-fu.

[1] For such errors in Lectionary notices, see my *Early Syriac Lectionary System*, p. 15.

INDEX

INDEX

Flügel, G., 6, 15, 26, 26 n., 50, 60 n., 72 n., 74, 84 f., 89, 94, 105 f., 107, 109 f.
Food, 23, 47, 56, 60 n.
Fortunatus, 46 n.
Friend of Luminaries, 26
Futtak, Fātik. *See* Patticius

George and Dragon, 29 n.
God, Manichee doctrine of, 19, 33, 39 f., 50, 61
Green, Canon P., 69, 100
Gunde-Shapur, 5

Hearers, 44 f., 55, 59, 83, 105
Hermas, 96, 125
Hermes, Trism., 38, 96
Hierotheos, 26 n.
Hill, G. F., 8 n.
Huxley, T. H., 81
Hyle, 95
Hypodectae, 95

Irenaeus, 23, 102
Israel, 88, 91

Jacob (angel). *See* Prēstags
Jesus, in Manichee theology, 37–43, 90, 92 f.
Friend, 31
patibilis, 31 n., 42 n., 111
Zīwānā, 31, 111
Julia, Manichee, 8 ff.

Kashkar (Wāsit), 14 n.
Khormuzta. *See* Ormuzd
Khuastuanift, 16, 25 n., 48–63, 108, 109, 110
Kings of Glory and Honour, 28
Kphalpālā, 106
Kugener, M. A., 19 n.

Le Coq, A. von, 16, 48, 52 n., 97.
See also p. 130
Living Spirit, the, 26, 28

Maḥistag, 105. *See* Presbyter
Manāstār ḥīrza, 48, 52 ff.
Mani, Manichees, *passim*
Marcion, 14, 41, 75, 80 ff., 86
Margoliouth, D. S., 73 n., 115 ff.
Mark the Deacon, 7 ff.
Mayor, J. E. B., 19 n.
Messenger, the, 29 f., 38, 40
Milton, 19, 103
Mitchell, C. W., 13 n. *See* Ephraim
Mixture, 4, 17, 21, 23, 30, 63, 78, 100
Moments, Three, 17, 55
Monday, 57
Moses b. Kepha, 76
Mother of Life, 22 f., 40
Müller, F. W. K., 16. *See* p. 130

Nadīm, an-. *See* Flügel
Naḥashbat, 25
Nestorians, 85, 119–125
Nom, 53 n.

Ormuzd, 50, 51, 52 n., 86

Paraclete (Mani), 43, 94
Patticius, 21, 32, 66, 82
Pelliot, Paul, 16
Peter, Gospel of, 87
Plato, 38
Porphyry of Gaza, 7 ff.
Pragmateia, 32, 66
Pravaḥr, 25, 107, 110
Presbyter, 46 n., 105
Prēstags, 30, 50, 53, 90
(=angels), 91
Primal Man, 22–27, 40, 50

Radloff, W., 48
Roots, Two, 17, 55, 88
Rōshan-rahē, 108

Safsēr, 93
Sanctus, 92

INDEX

INDEX

CAMBRIDGE: PRINTED BY W. LEWIS AT THE UNIVERSITY PRESS

For EU product safety concerns, contact us at Calle de José Abascal, 56–1°, 28003 Madrid, Spain or eugpsr@cambridge.org.

 www.ingramcontent.com/pod-product-compliance
Ingram Content Group UK Ltd.
Pitfield, Milton Keynes, MK11 3LW, UK
UKHW012339130625
459647UK00009B/392